A NEW APPROACH

SECOND EDITION

Buddhism

Steve Clarke

HODDER
EDUCATION
www.hod...........co.uk

A note on the spelling of religious terms

Buddhist concepts are traditionally expressed in either the Pali or Sanskrit languages. Pali is usually associated with Theravada Buddhism, and Sanskrit with the Mahayana sects, including Vajrayana. This convention has been followed in the book, with Pali being the default spelling (unless the conventional spelling is Sanskrit!). Thus, for example, the Buddha is referred to as Siddattha Gotama, except in the context of Mahayana Buddhism, where the name is spelt Siddhartha Gautama. Words specific to Japanese or Tibetan Buddhism are transliterated from those languages. In the Key Words sections at the beginning of each Unit, direct translations of Buddhist terms are given in inverted commas.

The Publishers would like to thank the following for permission to reproduce copyright material:
AKG Images/Robert O'Dea: p. 46; AKG Images/The British Library Ms. Oriental: p. 110 (top); © Paul Almasy/CORBIS: p. 6; © Tony Arruza/CORBIS: p. 13; The Art Archive/Musée Guimet Paris/Dagli Orti: p. 113 (right); © Bass Museum of Art/CORBIS: p. 96; Steve Clarke: p. 92; © B.S.P.I/CORBIS: p. 34; The Buddhist Hospice Trust for their logo: p. 137; © Clouds Hill Imaging Ltd./CORBIS: p. 135; COREL Royalty Free Disc: pp. 60, 63, 64, 97, 128, 140; © David Cumming; Eye Ubiquitous/CORBIS: pp. 73, 75, 88; Deer Park Monastery, Plum Village www.plumvillage.org: p. 125; © Macduff Everton/CORBIS: pp. 91 (top), 103; © Owen Franken/CORBIS: p. 32; © Louise Gubb/CORBIS SABA: p. 40; *The Heart Sutra* by Geshe Sonam Rinchen (Snow Lion Publications, 2003): p. 111; ©Lindsay Hebberd/CORBIS: pp. 91 (bottom), 113 (left); © Robert van der Hilst/CORBIS: p. 14; © John Hulme; Eye Ubiquitous/CORBIS: p. 54 (top); © Hanan Isachar/CORBIS: p. 53; © Christine Kolisch/CORBIS: p. 54 (bottom); © Craig Lovell/CORBIS: p. 3; © Colin McPherson/CORBIS: pp. 51, 89; Moksajyoti/Clear Vision Trust: p. 47; Kevin R. Morris/CORBIS: p. 62; PA Photos/EPA: p. 68; © Tim Page/CORBIS: pp. 31, 132; Photodisc Royalty Free Disc: pp. 2, 14, 55, 67, 86, 93, 97, 128; Rex Images/John Powell: p. 128 (bottom, centre); © Carmen Redondo/CORBIS: p. 86 (left); © Reuters/CORBIS: p. 54 (middle); River Publications, Aruna Ratanagiri Buddhist Monastery: p. 45; David Rose: pp. 71, 122; © Sakamoto Photo Research Laboratory/CORBIS: pp. 38, 76; © ML Sinibaldi/CORBIS: p. 130; © Luca I. Tettoni/CORBIS: p. 93 (left); Topham: p. 110 (bottom); © Brian A. Vikander/CORBIS: p. 81; © Alison Wright/CORBIS: pp. 39, 90.

Associated Press, extract from 'Thousands of Hindus convert to Buddhism in India racism protest', 10 September 2001; BMJ Publishing Group Ltd., extract from 'Buddhism, euthanasia and the sanctity' by RW Perrett, *Journal of Medical Ethics*: 22(5) 1996, pp. 309–314; Buddha Dharma Education Association Inc, extract from *Milinda Panha* (adapted), extract from *Diamond Sutra* (adapted); Buddhist Publication Society, extract from *Maha-parinibbana Sutta* (adapted), 1998, extract from *Jataka*, 1996, extract from *The Sutta* from Anguttara Nikaya; Buddhist Text Translation Society, extract from Avatamsaka Sutra (adapted); Dhamma Dana Publications, extracts from Dhammapada (adapted); Dhammakaya Foundation, extract from 'Brahma Sahampati' from *Ariyapariyesana Sutta* (adapted); Dharma Haven, extract from *Advice on the Benefits of Prayer Wheels* by Lama Zopa, Rinpoche, given at Land of Medicine Buddha, June 1994 © Dharma Haven 1997; FWBO Communications Office, extract from www.fwbo.org; Go2Nepal.com, extract from a speech by the Dalai Lama, www.go2nepal.com/d-lama.html © 1996–2004; *Lanka Daily News*, extract from 'Appeal of Buddhism in the West' by Radhika Abeysekera, 13 August 2003; Nattawud Daoruang, extract from www.thailandlife.com/monk.html by Nattawud Daoruang; The Office of Tibet, extract from a speech by the Dalai Lama's Nobel lecture at University Aula, Oslo, 11 December 1989, www.tibet.com/DL/nobellecture.html; Pan Macmillan, extract from *Siddhartha* by Herman Hesse (adapted), 1976; The Sangha, Bung Wai Forest Monastery, quotations from Ajahn Chah from Bodhinyana, 1982; Snow Lion Publications, page from *The Heart Sutra* by Geshe Sonam Rinchen, © 2003 Ruth Sonam, www.SnowLionPub.com; SpiritSound, extract from a speech by the Dalai Lama in India, www.spiritsound.com/bhikshu.html; *The Sunday Times*, extract from article by Simon Blackburn, 4 April 2004; Thanissaro Bhikkhu, extract from *Introduction to the Patimokkha Rules* by Thanissaro Bhikkhu, 1994; *The Times*, extract from 'Hoddle says disabled are paying for sins of previous life' by Matt Dickenson and Stephen Farrell, 30 January 1999, © NI Syndication, London; West Covina Buddhist Temple, quotation from Thich Nhat Hahn, www.livingdharma.org © West Covina Buddhist Temple, 1997–2004.

Every effort has been made to trace all copyright holders, but if any have been inadvertently overlooked the Publishers will be pleased to make the necessary arrangements at the first opportunity.

Although every effort has been made to ensure that website addresses are correct at time of going to press, Hodder Education cannot be held responsible for the content of any website mentioned in this book. It is sometimes possible to find a relocated web page by typing in the address of the home page for a website in the URL window of your browser.

Orders: please contact Bookpoint Ltd, 130 Milton Park, Abingdon, Oxon OX14 4SB. Telephone: (44) 01235 827720. Fax: (44) 01235 400454. Lines are open from 9.00–5.00, Monday to Saturday, with a 24-hour message answering service. Visit our website at www.hoddereducation.co.uk.

© Steve Clarke 2005
First published in 2005 by
Hodder Education, an Hachette UK company
338 Euston Road
London NW1 3BH

Impression number 10 9 8 7 6
Year   2011

Cover photo courtesy of Jeremy Horner/CORBIS
Typeset in 10.5 on 13pt Berling by Phoenix Photosetting, Lordswood, Chatham, Kent
Printed in Dubai

A catalogue record for this title is available from the British Library

ISBN-13: 978 0 340 81505 2

Contents

A New Approach – Buddhism

UNIT ONE | Buddhist Beliefs

KEY WORDS

Anatta: No independent or permanent self.

Anicca: The impermanent nature of all things.

Buddha: 1. One who is fully awake or enlightened; 2. Siddattha Gotama.

Dhamma: 1. The universal law of life; 2. The teachings of the Buddha.

Dukkha: Suffering, unsatisfactoriness.

Enlightenment: The state of having developed the wisdom to see life as it really is.

Five Khandhas: The five elements that make up a human being.

Four Noble Truths: Suffering; the cause of suffering; the end of suffering; the way to end suffering.

Four Sights: Old age; sickness; death (i.e. suffering); a holy man (i.e. the determination to overcome suffering).

Kamma: 1. Actions that influence one's future; 2. The law of cause and effect.

Nibbana: The state of peace achieved when suffering and its causes are overcome.

Noble Eightfold Path: Eight steps towards overcoming desires and reaching Nibbana.

Samsara: 1. The ordinary, ever-changing world; 2. The cycle of rebirths.

Tanha: Desire, craving, wanting.

Three Poisons: The causes of human unhappiness: greed, hatred, ignorance.

Three Universal Truths: The characteristics of life: anicca, anatta, dukkha.

KEY QUESTION

Who was the Buddha?

WHAT IS A BUDDHA?

A **buddha** is an enlightened human being. This means someone who has come to understand the true nature of life.

Most people know very little about life. Some may know a lot about how it works, but few know about why. Many people believe that their life has meaning or purpose, but few can explain easily what it is. A person who has reached a deep understanding of these things is said to be enlightened: a buddha.

From this, two things follow. First, each of us has the capacity or potential to discover the truth about life and be a buddha. We all have the capacity to become angry or jealous or generous, and we show these qualities from time to time, given the right circumstances and stimuli. In the same way, Buddhists believe that everyone has a buddha nature – the potential to be enlightened. The practice of Buddhism is aimed at bringing it out.

Secondly, if anyone can become a buddha, presumably there have been buddhas in the past, there are buddhas today, and there will be buddhas in the future. If this is the case, who was the person known as the Buddha, and what makes him special?

WHO WAS THE BUDDHA?

When Buddhists talk about the Buddha, they are generally referring to Siddattha Gotama (Siddhartha Gautama – Sanskrit), the first buddha in history to have his life and teachings recorded.

Siddattha lived in northern India, and spent most of his life teaching in the cities of the Ganges plain. The usual dates given for his life are from 563 to 483 BCE, although some modern scholars have suggested that he might have lived about a century later.

The organised religion of that time was what we now call Hinduism. But then, as now, there was no single Hindu religion, just a great variety of Indian religious traditions and practices.

The Brahmins, that is the priests, had a strong influence on the formal religion of the day. But they were not the only source of religious ideas, for there were wandering, freelance religious teachers, each of whom would attract a number of followers, who would provide them with life's necessities. They would travel from place to

▲ A buddha is an ordinary human being who is enlightened.

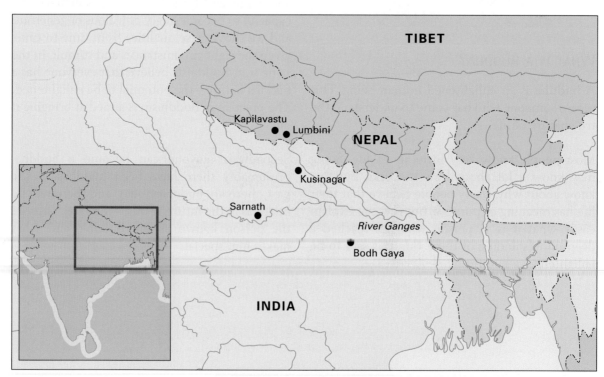

▲ Northern India showing places associated with the life of Siddattha.

place teaching, and people would offer them food in return. When Siddattha became enlightened and started to travel around preaching, he was seen as one of a large number of such wandering preachers. They were called sadhus. In general, the sixth and fifth centuries BCE seem to have been a time when the people of the Ganges plain were asking religious questions and willing to explore new ideas, and the sadhus responded to this interest.

How do we know about Siddattha?

For about 600 years, stories about the Buddha were passed on by word-of-mouth. They were told in order to illustrate his teachings and inspire his followers. The earliest written account of his life comes from about 100 CE.

Because they were told for religious reasons, the stories about the Buddha have religious signifi-cance and may not all be historical fact. Some of them have been elaborated into myths, as is usual with stories of great religious leaders. They express the devotion of his followers.

We do know, however, that Siddattha existed, and that he spent about 45 years travelling and teaching in northern India, dealing with people's individual problems, developing his teachings and spiritual practices to suit the people he met, and organising his followers, many of whom became wandering teachers like himself.

TEST YOURSELF

1 What does 'enlightenment' mean?
2 How long ago did the Buddha live?
3 What facts are known about the Buddha's life?
4 Why were some stories about the Buddha made up?

▲ In the Hindu tradition, sadhus still devote their lives to a search for spiritual enlightenment.

What stories are told about Siddattha's birth and early life?

KEY QUESTION

Why is Siddattha important for Buddhists today?

Siddattha Gotama was born in a place called Lumbini, in the foothills of the Himalayas. His family was one of a number of leading families who governed the tribal groups of that part of India. Indeed, Siddattha is sometimes known as Shakyamuni, which means 'wise man of the Shakya clan', to show his princely status.

His father was Raja Shuddhodana of the Kingdom of Kapilavatsu; his mother was Queen Maya. In the story of Siddattha's birth, his mother dreamed that an elephant with six tusks and a head the colour of rubies came down from the highest heaven to enter her womb through her right side. Eight Brahmins (priests) told the King that this dream was a good omen, and that the child would be holy and achieve perfect wisdom.

▲ The story of the birth of Siddattha is full of religious imagery.

Queen Maya entered the garden at Lumbini accompanied by her dancing women and her guards, and walked beneath a sala tree. The tree bent down and the Queen took hold of it and looked up to the heavens. At that point Siddattha, the future Buddha, was born out of her side as she stood beneath the tree. He immediately took seven steps towards each quarter of heaven, and at each of these steps there sprung up a lotus flower. He then declared that he would have to experience no more births, that this was his last body and that he would pluck out by the roots the sorrow caused by birth and death.

Queen Maya died seven days after Siddattha's birth, and he was brought up by his aunt, Mahapajapati Gotami, who was also married to his father.

Siddattha would have been expected to follow his father, and take his place as head of the family and as a local ruler. There is a tradition that, at his birth, a seer called Asita predicted that he would become either a great ruler or a religious teacher. His father was anxious that he should rule. He was afraid that, if his son took an interest in spiritual matters and questions about the meaning of life, he would become too interested in religion. So he tried to keep all knowledge of what life was like for ordinary people from the boy, and kept him in the lavish surroundings of the palace complex.

By all accounts, Siddattha was a very gifted young man, equally talented in the sports and the arts. He enjoyed a luxurious lifestyle, including a staff of young women to keep him amused. At the age of 16 he was married to a local 'princess' called Yasodhara, and they had a son, Rahula.

TEST YOURSELF

1 Where did Siddattha live?
2 What does 'Shakyamuni' mean?
3 Why did Siddattha's father not want him to be a religious teacher?
4 Why did Siddattha's father protect him from knowledge about real life?

How did Siddattha find out about ordinary life?

Although Siddattha's father tried to prevent his son from developing religious interests, the young man was deeply curious about the world around him, and he grew dissatisfied that he was not able to explore beyond the palace. Yet, in spite of his father's efforts to protect him from the realities of life, he saw four things while riding out with his charioteer, Channa, that changed his life. They have become known as the **Four Sights**, of which the first three are:

- An old man.
- A sick person.
- A corpse.

These are all examples of suffering that no one can avoid. They are part of life. At this point Siddattha is described as losing his taste for life. He was no longer able to enjoy all the luxuries of his life knowing that they could not protect him from old age, sickness and death.

Then Siddattha saw:

- A holy man.

This was a sadhu, a man who devotes his life to the spiritual path. This fourth sight led Siddattha to decide that he, too, would leave home and become a sadhu in order to seek a cure for the world's suffering. Once he had seen the facts about life and the scope of human suffering, he felt compelled to do something about it.

▲ When Siddattha was a young man he saw four things when he was riding out (these are now known as the Four Sights). Seeing a sadhu inspired Siddattha to become a seeker of the truth.

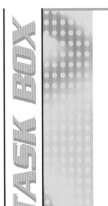

TASK BOX

Explain why Buddhists are not concerned about the historical accuracy of stories about the Buddha.

In your answer you should refer to:
- what Buddhists believe about enlightenment
- the belief that all people can become enlightened
- the significance of the Buddha for his followers
- some of the stories
- the possibility that something can be true without being historical.

Siddattha's search for the truth

To start with, Siddattha went to two different religious teachers and trained in meditation, but he failed to find the solution to suffering that he sought. He therefore went into the forest and joined a group of ascetics. These were sadhus who tried to achieve spiritual benefit from living very simply and from treating the body with the strictest discipline. They attempted to overcome suffering by deliberately exposing themselves to it.

For six years Siddattha followed this way of life. He assumed that the only way to become spiritually enlightened was to reduce his physical needs to an absolute minimum. It is said that, in doing this, he nearly starved himself to death, surviving on just one grain of rice a week.

One day he went to bathe in the river and, as he came out of the water, he saw a young cowgirl who offered him a bowl of milk-rice. Siddattha realised that his ascetic practices could never lead him to full insight. He had become too weak even to meditate. So he accepted the food. His fellow ascetics thought that he was going to return to his life of luxury. Disappointed at his apparent failure, they deserted him. But Siddattha had learnt an important lesson. He had discovered that his extravagant lifestyle could not protect him from suffering and so could not bring him deep and lasting happiness. Yet his ascetic existence brought him no closer to spiritual fulfilment. He realised that he would become enlightened only by living the Middle Way between the two extremes of luxury and hardship.

TEST YOURSELF

1 What did Siddattha learn from the Four Sights?
2 What did Siddattha decide to do as a result of witnessing the Four Sights?
3 What is an ascetic?
4 What is the Middle Way?

▲ Siddattha lived the life of an ascetic, but failed to achieve spiritual benefit.

▲ Siddattha accepted food and started to live the Middle Way.

HOW DID SIDDATTHA BECOME ENLIGHTENED?

Siddattha Gotama was 35 years old. He had experienced both wealth and poverty, and now lived the Middle Way. He sat in meditation beneath a pipal (fig) tree and determined that he would not move until he had achieved **enlightenment**. At first he had to struggle with temptations to abandon his quest, which came in the form of a 'devil' figure called Mara and his daughters. He fought against doubts that he could achieve his goal. Yet, after twelve hours of meditation, Siddattha became enlightened.

It is impossible to convey exactly what Siddattha understood as he became enlightened, because the understanding of it *is* enlightenment. You would have to be enlightened yourself to take it in fully. But we can see in general terms what he learned.

During his night of meditation, Siddattha gained knowledge of his previous lives, and how his past related to the present. He came to realise the way in which all things come into existence and pass away again; that all things are constantly changing. He saw how negative feelings and cravings make people grasp at life, even though it brings them suffering. And, as the sun rose in the morning, he experienced the peace of **Nibbana**, when all desires are overcome, and he became enlightened.

Mara is said to have demanded a witness to Siddattha's enlightenment. In response Siddattha touched the ground in front of him, and Vasundhara, the earth goddess, appeared to support the Buddha's claim on enlightenment.

▲ Siddattha sat under a pipal tree and meditated. The circle of light around his head symbolises enlightenment.

PERSPECTIVES

The book, *Siddhartha*, by Hermann Hesse, concerns the spiritual journey of a young man in India 2500 years ago. In the course of his travels, he meets the Buddha and hears him teach. In spite of the fact that many people join the Buddha's followers, the young man decides not to. This is how he explains his decision to the Buddha:

'I have not doubted for a single moment that you are Buddha, that you have reached the goal, the highest goal. You have found salvation from death. It has come to you in the course of your own search, on your own path, through thoughts, through meditation, through realisations, through enlightenment. It has not come to you by means of teachings! And – this is my thought, O Exalted One – nobody will obtain salvation by means of teachings! You will not be able to convey and say to anybody, O Venerable One, in words and through teachings, what has happened to you in the hour of enlightenment! The teachings of the enlightened Buddha contain much, they teach many to live righteously, to avoid evil. But there is one thing which these so venerable teachings do not contain: they do not contain the mystery of what the Exalted One has experienced for himself, he alone among hundreds of thousands.'

How do you think the Buddha would have responded to this statement?

What is it like to be enlightened?

As we have seen, there is a problem with describing enlightenment: to understand it, you would need to be enlightened yourself. But in the early writings of the Buddha's teachings there are descriptions of what it is like to overcome those things that prevent a person from moving towards enlightenment. They cannot describe what is experienced, but they suggest the sorts of feelings that arise when a person enters into deep meditation, and so give a glimpse of enlightenment.

Here are three of them:

1. Suppose you are a slave. Life is difficult: you are trapped, unable to go where you want or do what you want. You are limited by what others tell you to do. Then suddenly you are released. You are no longer controlled by others. You are independent. You are free.

2. Suppose you have been shut up in prison. You are not allowed beyond the four walls that confine you. Suddenly the doors are flung open and you are set free. You can return home; you feel safe and secure; you can start your life again.

3. Suppose you have had to borrow a lot of money to start up a business. Debts pile up and you have to work hard to pay them. Then suddenly the business takes off. Money flows in. You can pay off your debts and have money to spare. Your worries are over.

The feelings these scenarios express are of overwhelming joy, liberation, security and independence. We can assume that these are the feelings experienced by a buddha. They are accompanied by qualities of wisdom, compassion, courage, determination and sincerity. Enlightenment is not about 'understanding' in the narrow sense of understanding facts. It is a whole new way of seeing and relating to life.

TEST YOURSELF

1 How did Siddattha become enlightened?
2 Who was Mara, and what does he represent?
3 Why could Siddattha not be called the Buddha before his enlightenment?
4 Why is it difficult to describe enlightenment?

TASK BOX

Explain how believing in enlightenment might affect the life of a Buddhist.

Notice that the task does not require you to explain how enlightenment itself might affect a Buddhist's life, but refers to a belief in enlightenment. You will need to think about how our beliefs affect our lives and how we lead them.

What did the Buddha do after his enlightenment?

After his enlightenment, Siddattha can properly be called the Buddha. As a buddha, he now had to decide whether to keep his new knowledge to himself, or go out and teach it to others. At first he thought that others would not be able to understand it.

But, as one story has it, he was approached by Brahma Sahampati, the king of the Hindu gods, who begged him to go out and preach.

The Buddha recognised that some people were ready to benefit from his new understanding of life, so he decided that he would communicate to them the means by which they, too, could overcome suffering and achieve peace.

The first people Siddattha explained his enlightenment to were the Five Ascetics, whom he joined when he began his religious quest. He met them in the Deer Park at Sarnath, near Benares, where he taught them what he had learnt. As a result, they became enlightened themselves.

From then on the Buddha started to travel, teach and organise his followers. He had two types of followers. First, there were those who left their homes and families to wander, teaching others as they went. Second, there were householders who accepted the Buddha's teachings, but continued with their normal lives. This group is known as lay Buddhists.

For much of the year, the travelling followers went around the towns and villages of northern India, preaching and living off the gifts of food from the lay people. During the rainy season, however, it was difficult to travel, so the full-time followers would meet together for study and meditation. Some wealthy lay believers donated pieces of land to them so that they could have places to meet on a regular basis. As they spent more and more time at these places, so they became monks and nuns.

How did the Buddha die?

The Buddha spent 45 years travelling, teaching and giving others the benefit of his wisdom. At the end of his life, he had become the leader of a very large religious movement and was well known throughout northern India.

Finally, old and weak, Siddattha Gotama died of food poisoning at Kusinagar, surrounded by his followers. His body was cremated, but his bones remained unburned. There was some dispute about who should have them, but eventually they were distributed among the various rulers of the northern Indian kingdoms, who built monuments – stupas – over them.

▲ A stupa in the Deer Park at Sarnath today. It has become a pilgrimage site and is visited by Buddhists who want to understand more about the Buddha's teachings.

How do the events of Siddattha's life guide Buddhists today?

Buddhists do not think of the Buddha as a god, and he is not worshipped as such. But they do think of him as an important role model, as an enlightened being who devoted his life to the Buddhist path.

Siddattha's story provides an example of living the Middle Way. He rejected a life of luxury, yet saw that asceticism would not enable him to overcome suffering either. In working towards his enlightenment he showed determination and single-mindedness. He demonstrated the enlightened qualities of compassion, courage and wisdom in his dealings with others. In his religious life, he showed the practices that would lead his followers to become enlightened themselves.

TEST YOURSELF

1 How did the Buddha spend his life after his enlightenment?
2 What is a lay Buddhist?
3 What happened to the remains of the Buddha's body?
4 How is the Buddha regarded by Buddhists today?

TASK BOX

a) Explain the importance of Siddattha for Buddhists.

b) 'Siddattha is not a good role model for people today.' Do you agree? Give reasons for your opinion, showing that you have considered other points of view.

WHAT DID THE BUDDHA TEACH ABOUT LIFE?

KEY QUESTION
What do Buddhists believe?

The teachings of the Buddha are known to Buddhists as the **Dhamma** (Dharma – Sanskrit). Dhamma refers to what you base your life on. Your Dhamma could be football if that is what dominates your life and guides all you do. It could be music. Dhamma, for Buddhists, is the real nature of life, and a buddha is one who is enlightened to it. The Buddha did not invent the Dhamma. Dhamma has always existed, and Buddhists believe that the Buddha became awakened to it and taught it to others. Buddhists often prefer to call themselves 'followers of the Dhamma' because they use the Dhamma to guide their lives. So, Buddhist teachings are not just a set of ideas: they offer a way of thinking and acting that helps individuals to become enlightened themselves. The Dhamma is a practical tool to be used for a purpose. The Buddha described his teachings as being like a raft that a person uses to cross a river. It is something to be used and then set aside.

Doctors prescribe medicine to eliminate disease from the body. The teachings of the Buddha are prescribed to cure disease of the mind, to bring back its natural healthy state. So Buddha can be considered to be a doctor who prescribes cures for the ills of the mind. He is in fact the greatest doctor in the world.

Dhamma is that which can cut through the problems and difficulties of mankind, gradually reducing them to nothing. That's what is called Dhamma and that's what should be studied throughout our daily lives so that when some mental impression arises in us, we'll be able to deal with it and go beyond it.

Ajahn Chah

Read the two quotations by Ajahn Chah. What does Dhamma mean to him?

What is life?

In spite of all the discoveries humans have made about the science of life, we know very little else about it. We know that there is some connection between what we do now and what will happen in the future, but we don't really understand what it is. We can see certain threads that connect the past with the present, but we can't explain them. We have no idea why things happen to us, or what the future holds. In many important respects, we appear to have no control over our own lives.

▲ We can sometimes see how events in our lives are connected . . .

▲ . . . but sometimes we cannot understand why things happen to us.

Being enlightened means understanding and being in control of life at the deepest level. The Buddha said that in order to take charge of life, you must see it as it really is. Human beings learned to fly only once they understood about gravity. Then they were able to overcome it. In the same way, only by seeing life as it really is can you take command of it.

The Buddha taught that life has three characteristics or qualities. These are often called the **Three Universal Truths**. Sometimes they are called the Three Marks of Existence, because they mark out what life is.

Anicca   All things are impermanent; everything changes. All things that exist did not exist at one time, and all will eventually cease to exist. During their existence, they are constantly changing. In the time it has taken you to read this paragraph, you have changed. Your nails and hair are imperceptibly longer, some of your body cells have died and fallen away, and new ones have taken their place. Your thoughts and feelings are different. This is because everything is interdependent, everything interacts with everything else and so effects change in other things.

Anatta   Because things change from moment to moment, and because everything is interdependent, nothing has a fixed or permanent identity. A bicycle appears to be a thing in itself with an identity that we call 'bicycle'. But what if you take the saddle off? Is it still a bicycle? What if you then remove the handlebars? And the brakes? The wheels? The gears? At what point do you say, 'This is not a bicycle'? And at that point, how would you answer the question, 'Where has the bicycle gone?'? Anatta means that there is no bicycle, and never was. It is a label that we attach because it is convenient, but it is an illusion. In the same way, because there is nothing constant about you, Buddhists say that your identity is an illusion. Your body is made up of the things that it takes into itself: the air that surrounds you, the food that you eat, and so on. Those things become you. Your 'identity' merges with your environment and cannot be separated from it. You have no separate self. So Buddhists do not believe in the soul. In fact the word 'anatta' means 'no soul'.

Dukkha   Dukkha is usually translated as 'suffering', but it is more than that. Certainly it does refer to the unavoidable sufferings of life, like old age, sickness and death, but it also refers to the general fact that things tend not to go the way we want them to. Life is unsatisfactory. Let us say that you arrange to meet a friend outside a fish and chip shop at seven o'clock in a town with two fish and chip shops. At seven o'clock, you are outside one of them. Where is your friend? You've guessed it! It is just a fact of life that things go wrong. And how do you feel about this? You do not suffer, but no doubt you feel frustrated. You can never be permanently happy so long as this is the case. This is dukkha: 'unsatisfactoriness'.

▲ All things are connected. Ways in which we affect our environment come back to affect us.

▲ You can see change taking place throughout a person's lifetime – from cradle to grave. So, how fixed is your identity?

You cannot step into the same river twice.

Heraclitus

What does this saying mean in relation to the Three Universal Truths?

All this means that you cannot experience lasting happiness if you try to stop things changing and try to keep them as they are. You may imagine that this will make you happy, but actually it will only cause frustration. More positively, it means that if you accept things as they are, and let them develop as they will, then you can enjoy life to the full.

TEST YOURSELF

1 What do Buddhists usually call their religion?
2 What meanings does the word 'Dhamma' have?
3 How is the Dhamma like a raft?
4 What three characteristics does life have for Buddhists?

Who are you?

When we examined the idea of anatta, we saw that there is a sense in which there is no such thing as a bicycle. What we call bicycle is really just a collection of other things, put together in a temporary (impermanent) arrangement. It has no fixed identity. Buddhism says that this idea applies to everything, including human beings. Just like the bicycle, a human being is a collection of parts which themselves are subject to anicca and so will change. These parts are called the **Five Khandhas** (Skandhas – Sanskrit). (The word 'khandha' means a heap or a bundle.) They are:

- Form: the physical body.
- Sensations: the senses, through which we experience the outside world.
- Perception: the awareness of the information our senses give us.
- Mental formations/impulses: our reactions to the information we take in.
- Consciousness: the thoughts and feelings which make us aware that we exist.

The Five Khandhas are like five heaps of sand. Put them together, and you have one. They come together in a unique combination when a person is born, and they fall apart when that person dies.

TASK BOX

How might a belief in the Three Universal Truths affect a Buddhist's relationships with other people?

In order to answer this question, you will first need to consider the different types of relationships that people have, and then think about how the Three Universal Truths apply to each of them.

Why is life unsatisfactory, and what can we do about it?

If you have an illness and want to cure it, you need, first of all, to find out what caused it. Then you can attack the cause of the disease and so recover from it. The Buddha said that the same technique can be used to overcome the unsatisfactoriness of life. The method can be set out in four stages:

- The problem.
- The cause of the problem.
- The way to overcome the problem.
- Strategies to overcome the problem.

The four stages are called the **Four Noble Truths**.

1. All life involves suffering (dukkha).

This is the problem we need to overcome: the universal truth that life is unsatisfactory for everyone. Buddhism does not claim to be able to prevent you becoming ill, or getting old, or dying, but it does say that the practice of Buddhism can help prevent you from suffering from dissatisfaction with life.

▲ There are some things you just can't change.

2. The cause of suffering (dukkha) is craving (tanha).

The reason why we find life to be unsatisfactory is because we rely on things to make us happy, when these things are unreliable. They are unreliable because they are subject to anicca: they change. We want things to stay the same, but they don't: they decay and die. What causes us to suffer is not the things that we rely on for our happiness, or even the experience of pleasure, but the fact that we rely on them. **Tanha** refers to this relationship of reliance, of attachment. It means desire, wanting, craving. It will cause us dukkha because our actions are dominated by **Three Poisons**: greed, hatred and stupidity. These poisons are what cause us to grasp at things.

Greed refers to our desire to possess things and people in the belief that they will improve our lives. Hatred is a powerful emotion that ties us unhappily to others. Stupidity refers to our ignorance or illusion about the way things really are. When our actions are motivated by the Three Poisons, we end up suffering.

▲ Life would be better if only . . .

3. The way to overcome dukkha is to overcome tanha.

Quite clearly, if it is our desire for things that causes us to be frustrated with life, then we must overcome our desires. Then we can overcome our frustration. But a person who feels emotionally empty will want to grasp. Therefore the only way to stop craving is to discover inner satisfaction and an appreciation of life as it really is, to find happiness inside ourselves instead of relying on other things, so there is no need to grasp.

No thanks. I've given up.

▲ Our lives can be richer if we do not grasp at things outside ourselves.

4. The way to overcome tanha is the Middle Way.

A life of luxury is one of attachment, when we rely on things outside ourselves to bring us happiness. Yet we have seen that this will actually cause dissatisfaction in the long run. A life of hardship will cause us to crave and want those things that keep us alive. It, too, is a life of suffering. The Buddha said that the way to overcome tanha is to live the Middle Way, between the extremes of luxury and hardship.

NIBBANA

The point at which all craving ceases is a point of peace called **Nibbana** (Nirvana – Sanskrit). The Buddha is said to have achieved this state at his enlightenment. A person who has achieved Nibbana may still carry on living, eating, having relationships with other people (as the Buddha did for 45 years after his enlightenment), but his or her actions would be done from a selfless motive, not the Three Poisons, and so would not lead to further suffering.

Nibbana is not the same as extinction. Nor does it mean being so removed from life that you lose connection with it and feel nothing. Rather it describes a state of peace and happiness caused by the extinguishing of tanha. In fact, the word Nibbana means extinguishing, in the sense of putting out a flame.

Those who have achieved Nibbana still experience things that others see as pain or pleasure, but they do not respond to them in the same way. The experiences will not be the cause of further craving and suffering.

TASK BOX

Write a list of things that people commonly crave.

Before you read on, describe the kinds of things a person would have to do to overcome those cravings and attachments.

Think about the qualities they would need to develop, the actions they might take, the support they might need.

Then read the next section, and compare your answer with the Buddha's.

The Buddha's disciples needed further guidance. Living the Middle Way may enable you to overcome tanha, but how do you live the Middle Way? The Buddha gave various suggestions in response to this question. The best known is set out in the form of a path of eight steps: the **Noble Eightfold Path**.

▲ How does it feel when the flames have been put out?

TEST YOURSELF

1 What does 'Khandha' mean?
2 Why do desire and wanting cause us dissatisfaction?
3 What is Nibbana?
4 How can a person achieve Nibbana?

How can we overcome craving?

The Noble Eightfold Path consists of eight things a Buddhist can do to overcome tanha and so achieve Nibbana. Although the word 'path' implies a series of steps to be taken one after the other, the stages of the Noble Eightfold Path do not have to be done in any particular order, and can be done together.

The stages can be put together in groups where they share a similar theme:

■ The way of wisdom (prajna).
■ The way of morality (sila).
■ The way of mental training (samadhi).

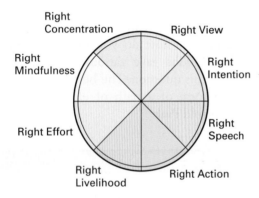

▲ The Dhamma is sometimes represented as a wheel with eight spokes – one for each of the steps of the Noble Eightfold Path.

THE WAY OF WISDOM

Wisdom is a characteristic of buddhahood. It involves true insight and a deep understanding of life.

Right (or Perfect) View

A Buddhist seeks to deepen his or her understanding of life by following the teachings of the Buddha. The right view of life is, therefore, the Dhamma itself. A person who has not thought about the nature of conditioned existence or the origin of suffering is unlikely to make progress towards enlightenment. Right View does not just mean learning about the Dhamma; it means accepting it as the basis of your life.

Right (or Perfect) Intention

It is one thing to hear or read about the Buddhist Dhamma, quite another to decide to act on it, and to do so for the right reasons. Right Intention refers to what motivates Buddhists to follow the Buddhist path. The motivation should be for the sake of a person's own freedom and eventual enlightenment, but also out of unselfish love for all beings. Right Intention is the driving force behind following the Noble Eightfold Path.

THE WAY OF MORALITY

Morality is about the right way that human beings should behave towards other people and their environment generally.

Right (or Perfect) Speech

In their dealings with others, Buddhists should avoid speaking to and about others in ways that would hurt them. They should avoid:

■ Telling lies.
■ Spreading gossip.
■ Speaking harshly.
■ Wasting time with idle chatter.

Rather they should always try to talk positively to and about others by:

■ Being sincere, careful and accurate in what they say.
■ Speaking in a way that promotes harmony between people.
■ Being kind and gentle when speaking to others.
■ Valuing silence when there is nothing useful to say.

Right (or Perfect) Action

All Buddhists try to follow a set of guidelines in the way they live. They are known as the Five Precepts. They are:

- Not to destroy or harm life.
- Not to take what is not given.
- Not to misuse sex.
- Not to lie (already part of Right Speech).
- Not to cloud the mind with drugs or alcohol.

(We shall examine the Five Precepts in greater detail in Unit Seven. There are other Precepts and rules for monks, and we shall look at these in Unit Three.)

Right (or Perfect) Livelihood

If a person follows the Buddhist path, it is important that he or she should earn a living in a way that does not go against Buddhist principles. Work should be of benefit to and should not harm others. (We shall examine this idea in Unit Eight.)

THE WAY OF MENTAL TRAINING

The last three stages of the Noble Eightfold Path indicate the spiritual practices that the Buddhist can perform in order to reach Nibbana.

Right (or Perfect) Effort

The first step in training the mind is to make a conscious effort to set aside negative thoughts and to replace them with positive ones. It is not expected that a Buddhist will manage this all at once! The key word here is 'effort': this stage recognises that a Buddhist should be aware of and be determined to shape the way he or she habitually thinks. In following this step, a Buddhist will always try to see the best in others.

Right (or Perfect) Mindfulness

Being mindful of something means having that thing right at the forefront of your mind; having your mind full of it. This stage of the Buddhist path aims to help people become more aware of themselves and everything around them. People cannot be in control of their lives if they are unaware of these things. It means starting to recognise unconscious motives and impulses as well as observing and responding to the needs of others.

Right (or Perfect) Concentration

This refers to training the mind through meditation practices. Buddhists believe that through meditation the mind is enabled to become calm, to develop loving kindness, and also to gain insight into the truths of life. (We shall find out more about meditation in Unit Five.)

TEST YOURSELF

1 What is the Right View of life for Buddhists?
2 How should Buddhists behave towards others?
3 Give one example of a job a Buddhist would not have.
4 What is the purpose of Buddhist meditation?

TASK BOX

Which steps of the Noble Eightfold Path do you follow already? Give examples.

Which of them would be the most difficult?

Are any of them more important than any others? Which ones? Why?

KAMMA

We have seen that it is a characteristic of life that all things change (anicca). But we know from experience that we have some influence over the way that things change. We can and do shape our future. In Buddhism this idea is called **kamma** (karma – Sanskrit) or the Law of Kamma. It can best be summed up as 'actions have consequences'. In fact, the word 'kamma' means 'action'. But Buddhists believe that the consequences of our actions are part of the actions themselves. Therefore, a person's kamma is the accumulated effects of his or her actions. This means that what we do or say, or even think now, will affect our future. Our lives at this moment are the effect of our actions in the past. Positive actions create positive effects, and negative actions create negative effects. Buddhists believe that when an action is made, the effect is determined at the same time. So at any point your life is a collection of things waiting to happen; things you have caused to happen. Therefore we are responsible for our own happiness. We are the product of our kamma; we are our kamma.

▲ The lotus plant seeds and flowers at the same time. For Buddhists this is a symbol of cause and its potential effect occurring at the same time: kamma.

Of course, even kamma is not fixed; it is constantly changing. It changes as the effects of our actions come about, and as we add more actions to it. It would be more accurate to say that we change our own kamma. The trouble is that people tend not to: they continue to create and recreate the same kamma. A person who bears grudges because of something someone has done in the past could be said to be making the causes for that relationship never to get better. On the other hand, a person who is able to forgive what has happened – accepting and understanding it – becomes free from its negative effects. Buddhists recognise that they have control over their lives, and exercise that control by making a conscious effort to create positive kamma by making positive causes.

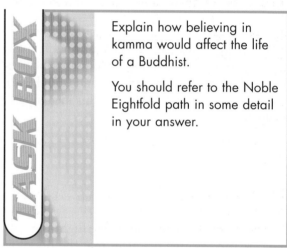

TASK BOX

Explain how believing in kamma would affect the life of a Buddhist.

You should refer to the Noble Eightfold path in some detail in your answer.

In the Dhammapada (an early collection of the Buddha's teachings), kamma is explained like this:

> Mind is the forerunner of all evil states. Our life is the creation of our mind. If one speaks or acts with an impure mind, suffering follows one as the wheels of the cart follows the ox that draws the cart.
>
> Mind is the forerunner of all good states. Our life is the creation of our mind. If one speaks or acts with a pure mind, happiness follows one as his own shadow that never leaves.
>
> *Dhammapada 1, 2*

TEST YOURSELF

1 What does the word 'kamma' literally mean?
2 What does kamma mean for Buddhists?
3 How does Buddhism explain why things happen to you?
4 According to Buddhism, how can you make your life happy in the future?

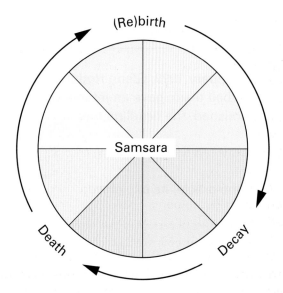

▲ Kamma moves from lifetime to lifetime in the wheel of Samsara.

Where does kamma go?

Buddhism grew in a culture of Hindu ideas and used some of these ideas in its development. One such idea was that of **Samsara.** This said that the world was like a great wheel of life and death, with creatures constantly being born, growing old, dying, and being born again. It was a world of suffering and death from which it was hoped that a person might eventually escape. The Hindu belief was that everyone had a soul (atman) that moved on to inhabit another body after death.

The Buddha accepted this idea, but modified it. For Buddhists, life is a constant process of change. What a person will be later develops out of what he or she has been before. This is believed to happen throughout life, but can it go beyond this life?

We have already seen that the Buddha taught anatta – no fixed self, no soul – so how can there be rebirth? What is there to move from one life to another?

If we are constantly being re-formed as the result of our kamma, then, when we come to the end of our present life, there is likely to be a great deal of kamma – through actions we have done, words we have spoken – that has not yet produced its results. A Buddhist might say that this kamma goes on to be worked out in future lives, which are therefore linked to our own in that way.

Buddhists do not speak of 'reincarnation', but rather of 'rebirth' or 're-becoming'. This is because the word 'reincarnation' implies that at birth a soul comes to inhabit a new body. In the Buddhist idea of rebirth, the body is itself the product of kamma. Your actions determine all the circumstances of your birth: the family you are born into, your sex, the colour of your skin – all the this is kamma. Whether a person is born with great intelligence or a physical disability or into poverty or with good looks is all a matter of kamma. Some Buddhists go further and say that the last act of consciousness of one life leads on to the first one of the next, and that some people can remember past lives.

None of this means that if people are born into unfortunate circumstances it is their fault. It is simply their kamma. Whether it is negative or positive kamma depends on how they use it. It does mean, however, that your life is your responsibility, and no one else's. Buddhists believe that, whatever a person's kamma, everyone can live a life of fulfilment and inner happiness.

PERSPECTIVES

In January 1999, Glenn Hoddle, at that time the manager of the England football team, gave an interview to a national newspaper. When it was published, the headline ran:

'Hoddle says disabled are paying price of sin.'

In the article, he explained:

'You and I have been physically given two hands and two legs and half-decent brains. Some people have not been born like that for a reason. The karma is working from another lifetime. I have nothing to hide about that. It is not only people with disabilities. What you sow, you have to reap.'

There was a national outcry. Tony Banks, the Sports Minister at the time, said Hoddle was 'from another world'.

'I have listened carefully to Glenn Hoddle's views,' said Banks. 'They are totally unacceptable. If his theory is correct, he is in for real problems in the next life. He will probably be doomed to come back as Glenn Hoddle ... There certainly have been times this weekend when I was wondering what dreadful things I might have done in a previous life to end up as the Sports Minister in this one.'

What do you think?

Was Hoddle right in what he said?

Did he explain karma (kamma) correctly?

If you were Hoddle, how would you have explained your belief in kamma?

Did the newspaper headline accurately reflect what Hoddle said?

Did the newspaper headline interpret kamma correctly?

Was Tony Banks' response to Hoddle's interview a reasonable one?

How do you account for differences in people's circumstances?

TEST YOURSELF

1 Why is Samsara a world of suffering?
2 How does Buddhism explain why people are born into different circumstances?
3 What does anatta (an-atman) literally mean?
4 Why is it incorrect to speak of reincarnation in Buddhism?

Buddhists believe that a new life arises in a way that is influenced by the life that has ended. Most people have no idea what influence their kamma will have on their next life, but Tibetan Buddhists believe that their senior religious teachers (lamas) can choose the next life they will influence. A child that is believed to be the rebirth of a lama is called a tulku.

When a lama dies, the monks seek out his tulku through dreams and visions. When they have found him, they arrange tests to make sure of his identity. Sometimes the child is asked to select personal belongings of the dead lama from a pile of similar ones.

Some people think that they can remember something of their past lives. A young child, although not conscious of it, may have some sense of having been the old lama.

This is an account of two events that led some people to think that a child called Osel, born in 1985, was a reborn lama.

Osel was born in Spain to Buddhist parents. His name means 'clear light'. His mother had a dream about Lama Yeshe, who had died in America in 1984. She sensed that the lama was telling her not to grieve for him. At the same time, while she was thinking about Lama Yeshe, she found that she was pregnant.

One year after Osel was born, a lama came to see him and laid out five sets of prayer beads. The child looked at them, and chose a very plain set – which had belonged to Lama Yeshe – rather than the more brightly coloured ones that a child might have been expected to choose.

Osel was later taken to see the Dalai Lama, the leader of Tibetan Buddhists, in India. He was crying when he arrived at the room where he was to meet the Dalai Lama, but, on entering it, he suddenly became quiet. He toddled over to a table on which there were some gifts, and picked up a white flower that was to be given to him. Then he went over to the Dalai Lama, and tapped him on the head with it! These things led people to think that Osel was, in fact, the tulku of Lama Yeshe.

Do you find the story of Tenzin (Protector of the Dharma) Osel convincing? Or is it all coincidence? Is it possible that we have had multiple lives? And can dreams give us clues about them? Give reasons for your answer, and make sure that you have considered all the evidence, both for and against.

How do Buddhists picture Samsara?

Tibetan Buddhists represent life in the world of Samsara in the Wheel of Life.

Buddhists will look carefully at the Wheel of Life, like using a mirror in which they see aspects of their own lives reflected. Each image within the wheel represents one particular feature of life, and the wheel as a whole shows how they are connected to one another.

In the hub of the wheel are three creatures – a cockerel, a snake and a pig – which represent the Three Poisons – greed, hatred and stupidity, respectively. Each bites another's tail, suggesting that they feed on one another. The world of Samsara is kept turning by these three things, since they motivate our cravings and attachments. Buddhists see them as the starting point of all human problems.

Outside the hub is a circle that is divided in two. On one side men and women, in various states of unhappiness and torment, are falling downwards. On the other, happy figures are moving upwards. This represents the changes that can happen in our lives as conditions (and our responses to them) change.

Next there is a circle divided into six segments, representing the Six Realms. These are not literally different worlds in which people live. They symbolise some of the emotional and mental states that humans find themselves in from time to time, states that dominate the ways that people think and act.

1. The realm of the gods. This represents the state of happiness that results from receiving the effects of positive causes. However, this is just a temporary state: it lasts only as long as one's positive kamma lasts.
2. The realm of asuras. Asuras are mythical war-like beings. They represent the state of anger, where you may be motivated by hate and envy towards someone, without realising that the hate and envy actually hurt you, too.
3. The realm of the pretas. Pretas are hungry ghosts. They have enormous stomachs with knives sticking out of them, and tiny mouths. No matter how much they eat, it is never enough: they have to have more. This represents the state of selfishness.
4. The realm of hell. This represents extreme suffering, the result of negative kamma. The suffering may be physical or emotional.
5. The realm of animals. In this state, a person is motivated by instinct for the basic requirements of food, sex and material comfort. People like this may be quite happy as long as their needs are met, but they lack civilising qualities, such as compassion, justice and foresight.
6. The realm of humanity. This is the state of being able to make choices: to create value or harm, to follow the Buddhist Dhamma or another dhamma. Only humans have these opportunities.

These realms, or states of mind, are not permanent. People move between them constantly, though it may be that one particular state may be foremost in an individual's character. If this is the case, that state will motivate that person to create and recreate the same kind of kamma in an endless cycle. This is Samsara: the world of suffering.

▲ In Tibetan Buddhism, people use the Wheel of Life as an object of concentration to focus their lives.

The outermost circle comprises 12 scenes depicting the Twelve Nidanas (Links of Dependent Origination). These illustrate the way in which one thing arises because of another, and therefore why the wheel of Samsara keeps moving round.

1. A blind man. He represents spiritual ignorance of the fact of anatta (no real self).
2. A potter at work. Because of ignorance, people make choices and start to create kamma.
3. A monkey climbing a tree. This represents the start of consciousness of a new life.
4. A boat with its passengers. This is the new body, along with its feelings, perceptions and acts of will (the Five Khandhas).
5. An empty house with six openings (five windows and a door or six windows). This represents the five senses and the mind, with which people are equipped.
6. A couple embracing one another. A person makes contact with things through the senses, and forms relationships with them.
7. A man with an arrow in his eye. Contact with things leads to feelings – pleasant, painful or neutral.
8. A woman offering a drink to a man. Feelings lead to thirst, or craving (tanha).
9. A man gathering fruit. People act on their cravings, making their attachments stronger.
10. A pregnant woman. Attachment leads to more life: 'becoming'.
11. A woman giving birth. 'Becoming' leads to the arising of new life.
12. A dead body. Everything that is born has to die, and the wheel of conditioned existence has completed its cycle.

In a visual way these links show that, as one life emerges, it develops senses. Then it makes contact with, and starts to grasp at, things outside itself. This grasping leads to the desire for more life, and the cycle starts all over again.

The Wheel of Life is held by Yama, the mythical Lord of Death. Yama is shown biting into the wheel, showing the relationship between life and death: everything that is born will die, and 'becoming' rises out of death. A Buddha is depicted in the top right-hand corner with his right hand outstretched, showing that the Dhamma is able to free people from the suffering of Samsara. The Wheel of Life represents the idea that there is a chance for people to escape from the endless round of life, death and craving.

TEST YOURSELF

1 What are the Three Poisons?
2 What is the connection between the Three Poisons and human suffering?
3 What are the nidanas? Describe them in your own words.
4 What causes the Wheel of Life to keep revolving?

WEBLINKS

http://www.chuavietnam.com/bstory/
Detailed biography of the Buddha.

http://www.ancientindia.co.uk/buddha/story/page01.html
Illustrated story.

http://www.acay.com.au/~silkroad/buddha/buddhism_philosophy.htm
Outlines the Dhamma.

http://www.buddhanet.net/e-learning/5minbud.htm
Questions and answers on the basics of Buddhism.

http://www.4truths.com
Interactive presentation of the Four Noble Truths (and the Noble Eightfold Path).

http://www.buddhanet.net/wheel2.htm
Interactive Wheel of Life.

1 a) Describe in detail Buddhist teachings about Nibbana and how to achieve it. (8 marks)
   b) Explain the changes a person might have to make in his or her lifestyle in order to follow the Dhamma. (7 marks)
   c) 'Only intelligent people can follow the Dhamma.'
       Do you agree? Give reasons for your opinion, showing that you have considered other points of view. (5 marks)

2 a) What is meant by the word dukkha? (2 marks)
   b) Outline the Four Noble Truths. (6 marks)
   c) Explain why Right Intention is important for Buddhists. (8 marks)
   d) 'No one can overcome suffering.'
       Do you agree? Give reasons for your opinion, showing that you have considered another point of view. In your answer you should refer to Buddhism. (4 marks)

Assignment

2

KEY WORDS

Arahant: In Theravada Buddhism, one who has attained Nibbana.

Bhikkhu (Pali), Bhikshu (Sanskrit): Buddhist monk.

Bodhisattva: 'Enlightenment Being', one who seeks enlightenment for the sake of all beings.

Dharmachari (m), Dharmacharini (f): An ordained member of the Western Buddhist Order.

Hinayana: 'Small Vehicle', a term used by Mahayana Buddhists for the Theravada school.

Kesa: 1. A robe worn by a Japanese priest; 2. A scarf worn by Dharmacharis and Dharmacharinis.

Koan: A word or phrase intended to bring about satori in Zen Buddhism.

Mahayana: 'Great Vehicle', the progressive Buddhist tradition of Eastern Asia.

Maitreya: The next Buddha for our world.

Mitra: A committed member of the Friends of the Western Buddhist Order.

Mondo: Rapid questions and answers to bring about satori in Zen Buddhism.

Nembutsu: Chanting 'Namu Amida Butsu' in Japanese Pure Land Buddhism.

Punna: 'Merit', fortunate kamma.

Sangha: 'Assembly'. 1. The community of Buddhists; 2. The community of bhikkhus.

Satori: 'Awakening', a flash of enlightenment in Zen Buddhism.

Six Paramitas: 'Six Perfections', virtues that lead a Bodhisattva to enlightenment.

Tantra: 'Pattern'. 1. The oneness of all things; 2. Techniques for visualisation.

Theravada: 'The Way of the Elders', the main school of Buddhism in South East Asia.

Trikaya: 'The Three Bodies', a way of explaining different aspects of buddhahood in Mahayana Buddhism.

Vajrayana: 'Diamond or Thunderbolt Vehicle', a type of Mahayana Buddhism represented by Tibetan Buddhism.

Vihara: 'Resting place', monastery.

Za–zen: 'Sitting meditation' in Zen Buddhism.

WHAT HAPPENED AFTER THE BUDDHA DIED?

> ### KEY QUESTION
> How did the first Buddhists organise themselves after the Buddha's death?

After the Buddha's death, it was feared that people would be tempted to worship him rather than follow his teachings. It was important, therefore, to compile an accurate record of his teachings. This was done by holding conferences of his original followers. The meetings were called Councils.

The First Council took place about three months after the Buddha died. Five hundred followers attended, led by three senior disciples. The three elders recited the Buddha's teachings as they had heard them. Once the whole Council agreed on the accuracy of them, they recited them together. However, they were not written down. In India at that time it was thought that writing down religious teachings debased them. They were therefore passed on by word-of-mouth. (People in those days developed a tremendous capacity to remember.)

The Second Council took place 100 years later. At this meeting the Buddha's followers discussed some of the rules and regulations laid down for monks and nuns. Some declared that they were too rigid to allow all people an opportunity to become enlightened. Others argued that observing the rules was the only way to attain Buddhahood.

The conflict was never resolved, so at the meeting of the Third Council, the community divided into two groups. Those who believed that the rules should be followed strictly formed the Sthaviras (the Elders), the forerunners of the **Theravada** school of today; and the more progressive members became the Mahasanghikas (Members of the Great Community), who laid the foundations of the **Mahayana** movement. Over the next 300 years or so, these two groups divided and subdivided until, by the end of the first century BCE, there were 18 or 20 Buddhist sects.

TEST YOURSELF

1 Why was it important to make a collection of the Buddha's teachings?
2 How were the Buddha's teachings agreed upon?
3 Why were the teachings not, at first, written down?

PERSPECTIVES

Buddhism spread throughout India and beyond during the reign of Emperor Asoka. Asoka was a bloody warrior, but became horrified by slaughter when he discovered and followed the Dhamma. Afterwards his reign was characterised by tolerance, non-violence and justice. He inscribed stones and pillars with Edicts which gave moral and religious guidance to remind his people of the Buddha's teachings.

Discuss as a group whether political leaders should allow their religious beliefs to influence their administration, or whether they should keep them private.

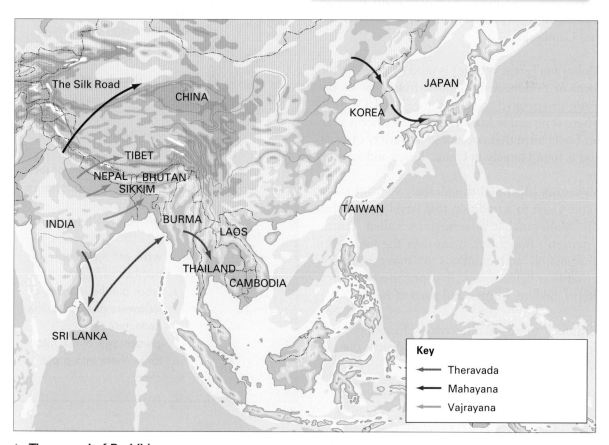

▲ The spread of Buddhism.

WHAT ARE THE YANAS?

KEY QUESTION

Why are there different branches of Buddhism?

As Buddhism spread, the many different groups of Buddhists moved outwards from India taking their particular traditions with them. Three different forms of Buddhism developed, called the Three Yanas.

Yana means 'vehicle' – something that helps you to make progress along your path. It expresses the idea that Buddhist teaching is something a person can use to assist with his or her journey towards enlightenment.

Hinayana (small vehicle) was the name coined by the more progressive (Mahayana) Buddhists to describe those who held very strictly to the monastic rules. This yana is represented today by **Theravada** Buddhism. It is the main form of Buddhism in Sri Lanka, Burma, Laos, Thailand and Cambodia.

Mahayana (great vehicle) is used to describe the form of Buddhism developed from that of the more progressive monks at the Third Council. There is no single Mahayana sect. Rather it is an umbrella term that covers a great variety of sects, and is found largely in China, Korea and Japan.

Vajrayana (diamond/thunderbolt vehicle) is the name given to a tradition that developed within the Mahayana. It is sometimes called Tantric ('pattern') Buddhism. It involves the use of the imagination and emotions to move a person towards enlightenment. It is practised in Tibet, Nepal, Sikkim, Bhutan and parts of India.

Although there are differences of interpretation and emphasis between the Three Yanas, they all agree on the following:

- Siddattha Gotama, the Buddha, as teacher.
- The Three Universal Truths.
- The Four Noble Truths.
- The Eightfold Path.
- Teachings about kamma and Samsara.
- The belief that there is no creator–God.

Although the three branches of Buddhism practise the Dhamma in different ways, each has the deepest respect for the others. There has never been conflict between them.

TEST YOURSELF

1   Why are the branches of Buddhism called Yanas?
2   Where is Mahayana Buddhism largely found?

TASK BOX

It is very difficult to calculate the number of Buddhists in the world, but the table below shows the rough distribution across the three branches:

Branch	Number of followers
Mahayana	185,000,000
Theravada	124,000,000
Vajrayana (Tibetan)	20,000,000

Represent the followers of the three branches of Buddhism in a pie chart.
To do this you will have to:

- work out the total number of followers
- work out the number of followers of each of the branches as a percentage of the total
- draw them into a pie chart.

WHAT IS THERAVADA BUDDHISM?

Theravada Buddhism grew from the original Sthavira school, and so thinks of itself as being closest to the Buddhism of Siddattha Gotama. At the heart of Theravada lie the Three Universal Truths and the Four Noble Truths. For Theravadins they imply that all life is liable to suffering, and that the Buddhist path is the way to escape from this life and, perhaps, after many lifetimes of practice, to achieve Nibbana.

A person who has completed the Noble Eightfold Path, destroyed attachment and the Three Poisons, and overcome dukkha is called an **Arahant** ('one who is worthy of respect'). To become an Arahant is therefore the goal of Theravadins.

▲ A Theravadin monk's robes are saffron yellow.

It is very difficult to become an Arahant, but it is easier for a monk (**bhikkhu**) to become one than a lay believer because the lay believer cannot devote as much time as a monk to spiritual training. So Theravada Buddhism stresses the importance of life in a monastery (**vihara**), and encourages every male to enter one for at least some time. In this way they have a sporting chance of becoming an Arahant.

Of course, in order to become an Arahant it is important to lead a good life so that you can generate good or positive kamma. What is good for one person to do in a particular situation may not be good for another, so a Buddhist will try to do whatever is most appropriate or 'skilful' in each situation.

A skilful act is sometimes called **punna** which means 'fortunate' since it will bring good fortune. In English, punna is usually called 'merit'. There are three kinds of action that are punna:

1. Moral conduct (sila).
2. Meditation (bhavana).
3. Giving (dana).

Any act of giving will attract good fortune. However, the amount of good fortune you will receive depends largely on your motive for giving. Therefore it is thought to be particularly fortunate to give in order to make someone else happy. It is considered less fortunate to give hoping to get something back, or simply to gain merit.

Theravadins believe that it is possible to enable others to receive the good fortune destined for you by transferring your merit to someone else. Better still, the transfer of merit is itself punna. The transfer of merit is particularly important when someone has died. On this occasion the family and friends of the deceased transfer merit to him or her and so encourage a fortunate rebirth.

Lay people can gain merit by giving donations to the bhikkhus. By giving in this way they can also transfer merit to a dead relative. A boy will gain merit by becoming a bhikkhu, and his mother will share this merit with him.

Explain how lay Buddhists of the Theravada tradition can gain punna.

You should relate punna to the idea of kamma, and explain how it can help on the path to Nibbana.

TEST YOURSELF

1. What is an Arahant?
2. Why is it easier for a bhikkhu to become an Arahant than a lay believer?
3. What is punna?
4. In what ways can a lay person create punna?

▲ Making donations to bhikkhus is one way for lay people to gain merit.

A New Approach – Buddhism

WHAT IS MAHAYANA BUDDHISM?

Mahayana developed from the progressive Mahasanghika group, though today it is not a single group, but a name that can be applied to a large number of Buddhist sects. Mahayana means 'great vehicle', in contrast to Hinayana, 'small vehicle', the Mahayanist name for the Theravada tradition.

Mahayana Buddhists do not disagree with the ideas of Theravada: they, too, follow the Dhamma (or Dharma, as they spell it), with the Four Noble Truths and The Noble Eightfold Path at its centre. But they build on those ideas to create a different outlook. They call their school 'great vehicle' because, they claim, their beliefs are more comprehensive and enable more people to benefit from them. Although many Mahayana Buddhists become monks or nuns, there is less significance attached to the monastic life. All believers have equal access to enlightenment, including lay people.

Whereas the Theravadins see the Arahantship as the ideal to be aimed at, Mahayanists have always claimed that this state is too limited. For them it is greater to become a buddha, and they believe that their teachings can and will lead people to buddhahood.

The idea that anyone can become enlightened led the Mahayana movement in about 300 CE to develop a theory about the nature of buddhahood and how the person of Siddhartha Gautama relates to each person's potential to be a buddha. It is called **Trikaya**. The theory is that buddhahood can show itself in a number of ways. It has three aspects, or 'bodies' (kayas):

- Nirmana-kaya (Transformation Body) The buddha nature can take on a physical form. This is the physical body that the Buddha uses to teach the Dharma to human beings. There are as many Transformation Bodies as there are enlightened beings in the universe. At death the physical body falls away, and the Buddha melts into the buddha nature of the universe. Some Mahayana Buddhists see great leaders of other religions, and even political movements, as Transformation Bodies of the Buddha.

- Dharma-kaya (Truth Body) The buddha nature is the nature of life, and is shared by all living beings. It consists of the enlightened qualities of wisdom, compassion, courage, determination, energy and the other characteristics that are associated with buddhahood. The Dharma-kaya might be called the 'buddha within'.

- Sambhoga-kaya (Enjoyment Body) This refers to the Buddha, or characteristics of the Buddha, that are seen in visions or meditation. While it is not a physical body, it is no way less 'real' than the other two kayas. It teaches the Dharma directly to people, regardless of time or geographical location.

It may be a little difficult to understand the idea of Trikaya at first, but it is an attempt to make the notion of buddha more accessible. It is sometimes compared with the moon to make it a little easier to grasp. The moon itself represents the Truth Body, that can be seen by anyone, anywhere in the world. It reflects into millions of lakes, pools, rivers and puddles across the earth. The reflections represent the Transformation Bodies of all the Buddhas who have ever existed in the universe. They are manifestations of the Truth Body. Anyone can then picture the moon in their mind; they can picture each of its various phases. These mental images are like the Enjoyment Body: we can picture aspects of the whole individually.

TASK BOX

Compare the Mahayana idea of Trikaya with the Christian idea of the Trinity.

To do this you will first need to research Christian beliefs about the Trinity. Then write down ways in which Trikaya and the Trinity are similar, and ways in which they differ. Remember: Trikaya describes the Mahayana belief about the Buddha; the Trinity describes the Christian belief about God.

In order to reveal the Truth Body, that is, to become enlightened, Mahayana Buddhists follow the Path of the **Bodhisattva**, whereby a person delays his or her own enlightenment for the sake of leading others to it.

▲ Mahayana monks and priests wear black or grey robes.

The word 'bodhisattva' means 'enlightenment being', and is a state of compassion, since it involves putting other people's interests first. There are four stages on the Bodhisattva Path:

1. Intention   A bodhisattva must be sincere in the desire to work for the enlightenment of others. Pure motivation is important on the path because it gives the bodhisattva determination to complete it.

PERSPECTIVES

A group of people was once travelling through a desert, when two of them strayed away and got lost. As time passed, and they parched in the desert sun, they became desperate for water. After many hours, their search came to an end when they discovered a well. The first man rushed to it, looked over the wall and found it full of pure, clear water. In his joy, he drank so much that he could not move. The second man walked over to the well, looked in, and then turned around and went back to the desert to search for his fellow travellers, to help guide them to this paradise.

What does this story teach about the Bodhisattva ideal?

To answer this question, you will have to think about what each of the following symbolises: the desert, the sun, the travellers, their thirst, the water, the man who drank from the well, the man who guided the others to it.

2. Vow   The Sanskrit word 'pranidhana' is usually translated as 'vow', but really it means 'fixation'. If you are determined to achieve something, the chances are you will. The vow itself states how difficult the task of the bodhisattva is:

> The deluding passions are inexhaustible: I vow to extinguish them all.
> Sentient beings are numberless: I vow to save them all.
> The truth is impossible to explain: I vow to explain it.
> The way of the Buddha is unattainable: I vow to attain it.

You do not have to be able to understand each line of the vow to work out that it is a promise to achieve the unachievable.

3. Practice This outlines the qualities the bodhisattva needs to develop. The practice consists of six perfections or achievements, the **Six Paramitas**:
   a) Giving (dana): selfless generosity.
   b) Morality (sila): thoughts, words and acts that are based on respect for all life.
   c) Patience (kshanti): accepting people and things as they are.
   d) Energy (virya): making effort to work for the benefit of all beings.
   e) Meditation (samadhi): clarity of mind.
   f) Wisdom (prajna): insight and understanding.
   (The Six Paramitas are described more fully on p.119.)

> Giving and morality make the foundation on which to build a great castle.
> Patience and energy are the walls of the castle that protect it against enemies from outside.
> Meditation and wisdom are the personal armour that protects one against the assaults of life and death.

Avatamsaka Sutra

4. Buddhahood The bodhisattva realises that the actions he or she has made in the service of other people are the actions of a buddha. In other words, the bodhisattva is a buddha all along. Taking the path is the way to understand this.

If a bodhisattva is a buddha-to-be, then Siddhartha (the Sanskrit – Mahayana – spelling of Siddattha) himself must have been a bodhisattva in his previous lives, before he was a Buddha. In fact, stories about the Buddha's previous lives were written down as the Jataka (Birth Stories). For some Mahayana Buddhists, therefore, Siddhartha is a superhuman Buddha. They believe that his powers over life are unlimited. In fact, the Japanese character for the word Buddha (butsu) literally means 'not a man'.

Mahayanists also believe that one day there will be another Buddha as great as Siddhartha, known as **Maitreya**. If this is the case, then the future Buddha is already in the world of Samsara. It could be your teacher, the person sitting next to you, or someone who served you in a shop yesterday. Mahayana Buddhists therefore believe that it is very important to treat everyone as though he or she is a potential Buddha.

These, then, are the general characteristics of Mahayana Buddhism. We must now look at some of the Mahayana sects themselves and identify what is unique to each of them.

TEST YOURSELF

1 Why is Mahayana Buddhism so called?
2 What is the Dharma-kaya?
3 What is a bodhisattva?
4 Who is Maitreya?

WHAT IS ZEN BUDDHISM?

The man who is credited with setting the character of Chinese Buddhism was called Bodhidharma. He settled in China from India in the sixth century CE. He claimed that the spirit of the Buddha's teaching could be summarised in four principles:

1. The teachings of the Buddha have been passed on by word-of-mouth exactly as they were taught.
2. The scriptures are not to be depended on as sources of the Buddha's teachings.
3. Buddhism points directly to the inner nature of human beings.
4. Since it sees into the inner nature of human beings, buddhahood can be revealed from within.

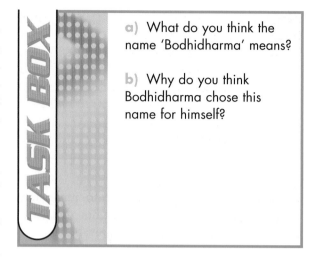

TASK BOX

a) What do you think the name 'Bodhidharma' means?

b) Why do you think Bodhidharma chose this name for himself?

▲ Bodhidharma set the principles of Zen Buddhism. He is usually depicted looking fierce and determined!

The way to reveal buddhahood is through meditation, 'jhana' in Pali, 'dhyana' in Sanskrit, 'Ch'an' in Chinese, and 'Zen' in Japanese. Zen Buddhism says that enlightenment exists within all human beings all the time. The aim of Zen practice is to become aware of it and awaken to it.

In the hustle and bustle of the modern world we have become obsessed with moving from one thing to another, with needing to know what will happen in the future. We do this so much that we rarely allow ourselves time to enjoy the present. One important aspect of meditation is that it enables a person to sit still and do nothing. The aim of Zen practice, then, is not to try to become a buddha or reveal one's buddhahood in the future, but to see it now.

The meditation practice of Zen is called **za-zen**, or sitting meditation, and is usually conducted in the lotus position. This means sitting cross-legged, with each foot resting, sole uppermost, on the opposite thigh. Sitting in the lotus position is important, for it allows the meditator to breathe easily and slowly, remaining awake, alert and aware. The amount of time spent on za-zen varies according to the time of year. At certain times it may go on for 16 hours at a stretch, interrupted occasionally to march around the floor to keep awake.

Zen Buddhists believe that we are all potential buddhas, but that we pile so much on top of our buddhahood – our worries, our lifestyle, our opinions, our ways of looking at the world, our ways of thinking – that enlightenment becomes hidden and difficult to find. The only way we can reveal our enlightened nature is to get rid of the things we put in the way. We have to abandon our traditional ways of thinking.

So, Zen abandons traditional logic and thinking and tries to get straight to enlightenment. When enlightenment comes, it comes in a flash, like remembering a forgotten name. This is called **satori**.

The ways to free the mind of traditional patterns of thinking used in Zen are the **mondo** and the **koan**. Mondo is a form of rapid question and answer that aims at speeding up thought processes until they are passed over, like an aircraft taking off. A koan is a word or phrase (often a shortened form of mondo) which cannot be answered by the ordinary mind. It is a riddle and a joke. It smashes through conventional thinking. A breakthrough of satori is required to solve it.

Here are some examples:

> Question: What is the Buddha?
> Answer: Three pounds of flax.

> Question: Is there a teaching no one has taught?
> Answer: There is.
> Question: What is the teaching no one has taught?
> Answer: It is not the mind and it is not the Buddha and it is not a thing.

> A temple banner flapped in the wind; two monks were arguing about it. One said, 'The banner moves.' The other said, 'The wind moves.' They could not agree. The master said, 'It is not the wind moving and it is not the banner moving. It is your minds moving.'

> Question: If I have nothing, what should I do?
> Answer: Throw it away.

> A girl is crossing the street. Is she the younger or older sister?

> Stand in the rain without getting wet.

How do you react to these examples? With frustration? With anger? That is because you are looking at them as sensible questions or statements. But they are not! They are designed to shock you. All of Zen is. They are nonsense – that is, non-sense. They make no sense. Nor does Zen. They take you away from logical sense into a world of satori. And how can you describe satori? You can't. Not with logical descriptions, anyway.

One Zen master said, 'There's nothing much to this Buddhism. Now that I am enlightened, I am just as miserable as I was before.'

TEST YOURSELF

1 What does 'Zen' mean?
2 Why do Zen Buddhists meditate?
3 What is satori?
4 What is a koan?

WHAT IS PURE LAND BUDDHISM?

Mahayana Buddhists believe that there are different Buddhas for different spaces and times in the universe, world-systems that are known as Buddha-Realms. Siddhartha Gautama (Sanskrit) is thought to be the Buddha for our world and age. The next will be Maitreya.

▲ Pure Land Buddhists devote their lives to Amida (Amitabha) Buddha.

The larger Sukhavati-vyuha Sutra tells of a king called Dharmakara who heard a sermon of the Buddha. He was so impressed that he left his kingdom and decided that he would become a buddha. He promised that, when he became a buddha, the realm over which he would preside would have the best qualities of all of them. It would be a Pure Land, where there would be no obstacles to enlightenment.

Altogether he made 48 vows concerning the Pure Land. They included:

- The promise that anyone who has vowed to be reborn in the Pure Land will be, even if they have made the vow only ten times.
- The promise that he would appear at the moment of death to anyone who had led a good life and worked towards entering the Pure Land.
- The guarantee that such a person would enter the Pure Land.
- The promise that a person reborn in the Pure Land could choose whether to complete the Bodhisattva Path and become a buddha, or return to Samsara and continue on the Bodhisattva Path.

It is said that Dharmakara attained enlightenment and, as a buddha, is known as Amitabha, which means 'Infinite light'. In China he is called Amita, and in Japan, Amida.

The purpose of Pure Land Buddhism is to be reborn in Amitabha's Realm of Bliss. Some Buddhists may see this as a literal rebirth in a universe called the Pure Land. Others interpret rebirth in the Pure Land as meaning the development of a pure (enlightened) mind and the qualities of compassion and wisdom, which are characteristics of Amitabha.

Being reborn in the Pure Land depends on three things. You have to really want it; you must have faith in Amitabha; you must create merit – positive karma – and dedicate it towards rebirth. One of the central practices of Pure Land Buddhism is to recite the Buddha's name by chanting 'Namo Amitabhaya Buddhaya' (Sanskrit) or 'Namu Amida Butsu' (in Japanese) over and over again. The phrase is called the **Nembutsu**, and it means 'I dedicate my life to the Buddha of Infinite Light'. Pure Land Buddhists believe that chanting the Nembutsu enables them to overcome attachments and dedicate fortunate karma to reaching the Pure Land (attaining buddhahood).

In addition to chanting the Nembutsu, Pure Land Buddhists read the Sutras, the books of teachings, especially the Sukhavati Sutras, which describe the Realm of Bliss in detail. This enables them to reflect on the qualities of Amitabha and develop them in themselves.

TASK BOX

'It is impossible to achieve anything just through positive thinking.'

Do you agree? Give reasons for your opinion, showing that you have thought about other points of view.

Pure Land Buddhists in Japan (the Shin sect) tend to concentrate only on chanting the Nembutsu. It provides hope to those whose lives are hard, and so became popular in Japan in the years following the Second World War. Today it is a practice that can be carried out by anyone, and is therefore suited to people who lead busy lives but still want to work towards spiritual enlightenment.

TEST YOURSELF

1 What is the aim of Pure Land Buddhism?
2 What is the practice of Pure Land Buddhism?
3 What is Nembutsu?
4 Why did Pure Land Buddhism become popular in Japan after the Second World War?

WHAT IS TIBETAN BUDDHISM?

The land of Tibet is, for the most part, over 16,000 feet above sea level. It consists of huge open spaces surrounded by towering mountains. The air is thin and the wildlife scarce. It would be hard to live in such a place and not think about the ultimate questions of life and death.

▲ Tibetan monks wear maroon robes.

For over 1000 years a particularly rich and colourful form of Vajrayana Buddhism has been practised in Tibet and the surrounding countries.

For centuries it was little known beyond the Himalayas, cut off from outside influences. Now it has spread worldwide. Since the land of Tibet was invaded by the People's Republic of China in 1950, it has been dangerous for Buddhists to practise their religion in that country as they would like. Many Tibetans, therefore, have left their homeland and settled in other parts of the world.

PERSPECTIVES

The Dalai Lama is the head of the Gelugpa (Yellow Hats) order of monks, and is seen as the spiritual and political leader of the Tibetan people. The title 'Dalai' means 'deep ocean', indicating that his wisdom is as deep and wide as the ocean. He was born with the name Lhamo Thondup, but his religious name is Tenzin Gyatso, and he is the fourteenth Dalai Lama. This means that he is thought to be the fourteenth human form of the bodhisattva Chenrezig.

Tibet was invaded by the Chinese in 1950, and by 1951 the capital, Lhasa, had been taken. The Dalai Lama was just 16 years old: the leader of his nation in a time of crisis. For some time, the Dalai Lama remained in the country, trying to compromise with the invaders. But in 1959, there was an uprising against the Chinese. The Dalai Lama realised that his life was in danger, and he and many of his followers fled across the border into northern India. He settled in a place called Dharamsala, at the invitation of the Indian government. From there he has worked to help the people of his country, and to make their troubles known across the world.

At first, after the rebellion, the Chinese tried to rid Tibet of the Buddhist religion. Many of the great and beautiful monasteries were destroyed and monks were killed. Since then, the situation has been changeable, sometimes easier, sometimes less so. There were even discussions about the possibility that the Dalai Lama might return one day. In 1994, however, in a further attempt to remove signs of his influence, the Chinese ordered that all photographs and paintings of the Dalai Lama should be removed from homes.

Since the invasion in 1950, it is estimated that 1.2 million Tibetans have been killed by the Chinese. The Tibetan language has been replaced by Chinese, and reference to Tibet's history and culture have been removed from the school curriculum. Today, more Chinese than Tibetans live in the region.

The Dalai Lama has said, 'The Chinese have done horrible things to us; they continue to do these things even now. But I still hold no hatred in my heart for them. Some Tibetans are very anti-Chinese and I do everything I can to restrain their urge to fight back. I do not believe in revenge.'

Is this a realistic way of leading an occupied nation? What might the Dalai Lama hope to gain? What, in his view, might be wrong with fighting back?

Tantric Buddhism

Tibetan Buddhism is a form of Buddhism that involves the emotions as well as the mind. In contrast to the simplicity of some other forms, its worship involves chanting and hand movements, special rituals, richly decorated robes and elaborate images. The name of this style of religious practice is **tantra**. Tantric ideas are found in Hinduism as well as Buddhism.

Following the Buddhist path is not easy. People who want to be Buddhists often find that there are parts of themselves that are very un-Buddhist – anger, greed, fear, or other deep emotions – and studying the Dharma does not in itself always remove these negative emotions. For that to happen, there has to be some way of getting in touch with these feelings, bringing them into the open, and then working to change all their negative energy into positive energy. So, for example, a person who is often angry is using up a great deal of energy in that anger – energy that could be channelled into wisdom, or into positive action.

Tantric Buddhism is the attempt to let Buddhism work on these deeper emotions. It consists of sounds (mantras), hand gestures (mudras) and various rituals, as well as visualisations, in which a person imagines that he or she is actually a buddha during a period of meditation.

When Buddhism arrived in Tibet in about 700 CE, it was already 1200 years old. By that time it included tantric practices, and this was the form that took root in Tibet. The religion that had traditionally been practised in Tibet up until that time was a very mystical faith called Bon. Buddhism adapted and mixed with Bon to form the Vajrayana tradition.

Eventually, Buddhism died out in India, so the Indian tantra disappeared. But this style of Buddhism was preserved in Tibet and neighbouring countries, just as Theravada Buddhism had already spread out and was being preserved in South East Asia, and Mahayana Buddhism further north in China and out to the Far East.

Gurus

A person cannot learn tantra unaided. He or she needs the instruction of a teacher, or guru (called a lama), and is given initiation by a guru. This means that he or she receives, with the help of the guru, the energy and insight needed for progress. It is like a seed – the guru gives it, but the disciple needs to take care of it and make it grow. Handing on traditions in this way is important, and Tibetan Buddhists speak of a lineage: a chain of gurus and disciples going back to the great teachers of the past. A disciple who has cultivated the seed can become a guru and implant that seed in others. It is hoped that the disciple will have learned everything that the master has to offer, and will then add his own experience – possibly becoming an even greater master himself in time.

Two of the best-known gurus from the past are Padmasmabhava and Milarepa (pictured below). Padmasambhava is regarded as the most important. He was the teacher who brought Tantric Buddhism to Tibet from India. He is therefore seen as the one who can interpret the Buddha's teaching so that people can experience it here and now. For Tibetan Buddhists he is therefore the most important person after the Buddha himself.

Milarepa practised black magic as a young man and killed off some members of his own family. Later he changed completely and became a Buddhist guru. All the energy that had been used destructively was channelled into doing good – but only after a great deal of effort in order to break his selfish and destructive impulses. By tradition Milarepa lived in a cave throughout the cold Himalayan winters, but, in spite of wearing very few clothes, did not get cold, for he used a special form of meditation that generates body heat. He is believed to have composed and sung many beautiful songs. Living in great simplicity he attracted a large group of followers.

TASK BOX

'In the practice of tolerance, one's enemy is the best teacher.'
Dalai Lama

Explain what the Dalai Lama means by this.

▲ The guru Milarepa, who channelled negative energy into doing good.

TEST YOURSELF

A
B
C

1 Which branch of Buddhism do Tibetans practise?
2 Why has Tibetan Buddhism spread abroad?
3 In what ways is Tibetan Buddhism tantric?
4 What is a lama?

HOW DID BUDDHISM SPREAD TO THE WEST?

KEY QUESTION

How is Buddhism practised in non-Buddhist countries?

We have seen how Buddhism started in northern India and spread out to the countries of South East Asia, Nepal, Tibet and the Far East. As it spread, it adapted itself to meet the needs of the people it encountered.

Skilful teachers know how to adapt their teachings to the needs of their pupils. Buddhist teachers have always done this, and, as Buddhism becomes established in the West it will gradually develop forms that are particularly Western.

Although some people in the West had heard about Buddhism, and Christian missionaries had gone to the East to try to convert Buddhists, it was not until the nineteenth century that Western scholars started to take an interest in Buddhist scriptures. In fact, the term Buddhism was coined at that time to describe all the religious practices carried out by those who followed the Dhamma.

By the end of the nineteenth century there developed a rather romantic idea of the Orient as a magical, spiritual place, a place of secrets and profound mysteries. Museums displayed Eastern art, including Buddhist images. It became fashionable to have oriental decorations, and the wealthy collected oriental art. Most people thought about Buddhism as something exotic and distant, unrelated to their own lives.

Although individual Buddhists had lived in the West, it was not until the second half of the twentieth century that people started to think of Buddhism as a religion by which Western people might live, and it was only then that Buddhist communities were established in the West.

There were several reasons for the increasing interest in Buddhism:

- People find it easier to move about the world today. There are many Thais, Burmese, Japanese, Tibetans and Chinese living in the West. They continue to practise their religion following the traditions they were used to in their countries of origin. They have built shrines and temples here in the same style as those in the East.

- Sometimes even war can spread an interest in Buddhism. After the Second World War, American forces were stationed in Japan; later they were involved in the war in Korea. This brought Americans into contact with Buddhists from those countries. During the Vietnam War, many American soldiers became interested in Buddhism, which they came across for the first time. At the end of the war, some of them wanted to continue to find out more about it. Others married women from Vietnam or Thailand and took them back to the United States. There were also refugees from the war who moved to the United States bringing their religion with them. This accounted for much of the growth of Buddhism in America from the 1970s.

- In the 1960s, Buddhist teachers started to come to the West. In particular, after the Chinese invasion of Tibet in 1959, Tibetan teachers (lamas) started teaching outside their own country, many coming to the United States and Europe.

- Since the Second World War, people in the West have experienced a freedom that they did not feel before. This extends to freedom of belief. People no longer feel an obligation to follow Western traditions just because they are Western. They are keen to try out new ideas, and this includes Buddhism.

- Some people have felt that Western religious traditions have not responded to the demands of modern life. They want to feel in control of the pressures that can cause stress and anxiety, and have turned to Buddhism because it offers the possibility of inner peace and happiness.

Several years ago the CBC radio programme, *Tapestry*, announced that Buddhism was the fastest growing religion in North America. By the middle of 1999, The Dharma Web Ring was the largest religious web ring in the world with the highest number of daily hits. America's fascination with Buddhism has spread to Hollywood and been translated into such movies as *Little Buddha*, *Seven Years in Tibet*, and *Kundun*. In October 1999, *Time* magazine was titled, 'America's Fascination with Buddhism'. It focused on celebrities such as Steven Seagal, Tina Turner, Richard Gere, Adam Yauchand and Phil Jackson, who had all adopted the Buddha's teaching and incorporated his teachings into their daily lives.

Radhika Abeysekera

Why do you think Buddhism is becoming so popular in the West?

HOW HAS BUDDHISM ADAPTED IN BRITAIN?

There are many Buddhists in the USA and in the rest of Europe, but if you visited a Tibetan, Zen or Theravadin centre in California, France or Germany it would not be significantly different from a centre in Britain.

There are more than 200 Buddhist centres and organisations in Britain. The numbers of people practising in them are divided very approximately as follows:

30%	Theravada
20%	Tibetan
15%	Friends of the Western Buddhist Order
15%	Zen
20%	Other Japanese sects (mainly Nichiren)

Theravada

The Theravada tradition in Britain has been led by Westerners who have gone East to train as monks, and then returned to establish monastic centres. The Buddhist Society of England was founded in 1906. At first it was an organisation that enabled people to learn about Buddhism, but very quickly it developed into the Buddhist Society of Great Britain and Ireland, a means for British men and women to practise Buddhism as a living faith.

In 1926, Anagarika Dharmapala founded a branch of the Maha Bodhi Society in London. Anagarika (which means 'homeless') Dharmapala was a Buddhist from Ceylon (today Sri Lanka) who re-established Buddhism in that country at a time when it was on the decline. He worked hard to make living conditions better for the people of his country, but was equally keen to spread the Dhamma in the West. So he set up the London Buddhist Vihara with resident monks from Ceylon, the first such centre outside Asia.

In 1967, Robert Jackman, a young American in Thailand met Luang Por Chah, a great teacher from the Forest Tradition. Monks of the Forest Tradition choose to live away from towns and cities so that they can practise the Dhamma through study and meditation. They live in the peace and tranquillity of forests. Under Ajahn Chah's tutelage, Jackman became a monk himself and took on the name Ajahn Sumedho. Sumedho spent ten years living in the forest with Ajahn Chah, and became the first abbot of a monastery for training Westerners. In 1977, they came to England at the invitation of the English Sangha Trust, a Buddhist centre in Hampstead,

▲ Ajahn Sumedho, founder of the first monastery of the Forest Tradition in Britain.

The monastery depends on gifts in order to keep going. It accepts these, and in return provides a point of peace, of meditation, and a place where people can go to learn to cultivate calm and contentment for themselves.

The monks at Chithurst (Cittaviveka) and Amaravati are Western. There are many other monks in Britain who come from traditional Buddhist countries and help Buddhists from those countries who have settled in Britain. For example, in London there is a Burmese monastery, a Thai temple in Wimbledon and the London Buddhist Vihara, which follows the Buddhist traditions of Sri Lanka. There are other Theravadin centres in Britain that are run by lay Buddhists (those who are not monks or nuns).

Zen

Zen is one of the most popular forms of Buddhism in America, but has a minority following in Britain. It became popular in the 1950s as a form of mental training that could be adopted by Westerners who might not be ready for the whole range of Buddhist teachings.

Most Western groups follow a tradition called Soto Zen. One such organisation is the Order of Buddhist Contemplatives (OBC), which has its European centre at Throssel Hole Abbey in Northumberland and now runs a number of other monasteries.

Tibetan

There are many Tibetan centres in Europe and America. The first to be established in Britain is called Samye Ling. It was founded in 1967 by Akong Rinpoche and Trungpa Rinpoche, though Trungpa left soon afterwards to start up another movement in the Tibetan tradition. This monastery and retreat, set in the Scottish borders, is the largest in the West. Monks from Samye Ling have set up the Holy Island Project, hoping that the ancient Western religious centre on Holy Island can be developed as a place of retreat for people of all faiths.

set up in 1956. Sumedho and two other monks stayed on after Chah returned to Thailand, and within a year it became clear that they should start a monastery of the Forest Tradition in Britain.

In 1978, supporters gave them over 100 acres of woodland in West Sussex, and they were later able to purchase a large house nearby, after the sale of the Hampstead centre. This became the Chithurst Monastery.

The monastery at Amaravati welcomes visitors. The monks and nuns lead meditation classes and give talks, as well as following their own studies and other work. Visitors are expected to follow the same routine as the members of the community.

The purpose of a retreat is to take a step aside from the demands of the world and spend time in reflection. Some Tibetans go into retreat for long periods. One group of Buddhists spent four years on retreat at Samye Ling, using their time to meditate and study. Although generally on their own, they did meet one another for meals. For a period of six months, they stayed in complete silence.

Other important Tibetan organisations are the New Kadampa Tradition (NKT) and the Foundation for the Preservation of the Mahayana Tradition (FPMT). The NKT's Manjushri Institute in Cumbria was founded by Tibetan meditation master Geshe Kelsang Gyatso Rimpoche. Its concern is to adapt Tibetan Buddhism to the West. The FPMT has a number of centres around the world, and is based in Britain at the Jamyang Meditation Centre in London. The FPMT is part of the Gelug tradition of Tibetan Buddhism.

Nichiren

Nichiren was a Buddhist priest who lived in Japan in the thirteenth century. He was convinced that the age of Siddhartha's Buddhism was coming to an end. He believed that a new form of Buddhism was necessary to bring people to enlightenment. This new form of Buddhism was based on the Lotus Sutra, a Mahayana scripture. Nichiren claimed that the Lotus Sutra was so powerful that simply chanting its title (Nam Myoho Renge Kyo) could reveal a person's buddhahood.

The Nichiren groups in Britain are dedicated to establishing world peace through their Buddhist practice. Nipponzan Myohoji has built 'peace pagodas' throughout the world, including London and Milton Keynes. Priests from this movement take part in demonstrations, work alongside other groups promoting peace and have daily rituals in which they chant for peace.

▲ Nichiren peace pagoda.

The largest group of Nichiren Buddhists in the world is called Soka Gakkai International (SGI) – the International Society for the Creation of Value. SGI is made up of lay Buddhists, not monks or nuns. Their organisation in Britain is known as SGI-UK, and it has its headquarters in Taplow, in Berkshire.

SGI claims that chanting Nam Myoho Renge Kyo can lead people to enlightenment, and can also change a person's negative karma (kamma – Pali) into positive. So these Buddhists believe that their Buddhist practice will bring positive benefits and success to their lives, including their work and relationships.

FWBO

So far we have looked at forms of Buddhism that have been imported into the West from the East. Many of their features are the same as you would find in their country of origin. But new forms of Buddhism have developed especially suited to life in the West.

The Friends of the Western Buddhist Order (FWBO) was founded in Britain in the 1960s by Dennis Lingwood. He had become interested in Buddhism as a young man living in south London, and became more involved when he was sent to India as a soldier during the Second World War. After the war, he stayed in India and became a Buddhist monk. He was ordained as a Theravadin, but later also studied under Tibetan and Zen teachers. When he became a monk he was given a Buddhist name – Sangharakshita – which means 'one who builds up the **Sangha** (the community of Buddhists)'.

▲ Sangharakshita, founder of the FWBO.

In 1964, he returned to Britain, and for two years he worked at the Hampstead Buddhist Vihara. He came to believe that a new form of Buddhism was needed for people in the West, a form that would use the earlier traditions, but make them relevant to the needs of Western people. He founded the Friends of the Western Buddhist Order in 1967 and the following year ordained the first members of the Western Buddhist Order.

The central feature of the Buddhist life, according to Sangharakshita, is 'going for refuge', which means devoting oneself to the example of the Buddha, following the Dharma and finding security in the community of Buddhists (the Sangha – see Unit Three). Those who are ordained into the Western Buddhist Order do not become monks or nuns. They do not make a distinction between monks and nuns on the one hand and lay believers on the other. Ordained people are called **Dharmachari** (male) or **Dharmacharini** (female), meaning 'one who advances in the Dharma', in other words, those who put the Dharma into practice in their daily lives.

At the same time as getting that title, the person who is ordained gets a new name. It may be in Pali or Sanskrit, and it generally reflects a quality that the person already has or that he or she is encouraged to develop.

Some members of the order live together in single-sex communities, while others live on their own, with partners or friends, or are married with families. Sangharakshita emphasised that commitment comes first and lifestyle second. In other words, a person has to make his or her commitment to the Three Jewels (the Buddha, the Dharma and the Sangha), and then the right way for that particular person to live will come about naturally as a result.

Members of the order wear ordinary clothes, but have a special scarf, called a **kesa**, to show that they have been ordained into the Western Buddhist Order. They wear it when they are teaching or leading worship.

The FWBO runs Buddhist Centres and retreat centres. People who attend these and start to practise Buddhism are called 'Friends'. Those who have been involved for some time, and want to support and develop their friendships with Order Members, may become **Mitras** ('mitra' is the Sanskrit term for 'friend').

Some Friends, Mitras and Order Members work together in team-based 'Right Livelihood' businesses. These provide a good environment within which to earn a living and also to generate money to support the work of the centres. In traditional Buddhist countries, local people offer financial support for their neighbourhood temple, but in Britain the FWBO relies on the income from the businesses and from the generosity of those who take part in Buddhist activities.

TEST YOURSELF

1 When was the term 'Buddhism' first used?
2 Why has Buddhism spread to the West?
3 What is the name of the main Nichiren organisation in Britain?

WEBLINKS

* http://www.dharmaforkids.com/Dharma/perfection/perfection.htm
  Try the Bodhisattva game.
* http://www.rider.edu/~suler/zenstory/zenstory.html *Some Zen stories and people's reactions to them.*
* http://www.forestsangha.org/index.html *The website of the Forest Sangha.*
* http://www.throssel.org.uk/ *The website of Throssel Hole Buddhist Abbey.*
* http://www.samyeling.org/ *The website of Kagyu Samye Ling Tibetan Centre.*
* http://www.kadampa.org/english/index.php *The Website of the New Kadampa Tradition.*
* http://www.fpmt.org/ *The website of the Foundation for the Preservation of the Mahayana Tradition.*
* http://awakening.to/schools.html *A brief summary of the main differences between the branches of Buddhism.*
* http://clutch.open.ac.uk/schools/willen99/tajinder/peace_pagoda/home_page.html *The Website of the Milton Keynes Peace Pagoda.*
* http://www.sgi-uk.org/ *The website of Soka Gakkai International in the United Kingdom.*
* http://www.fwbo.org/ *The website of the Friends of the Western Buddhist Order.*

REMEMBER

- The teachings of the Buddha were passed on by word-of-mouth for 100 years before being written down.
- The original purpose of the Councils was to agree on the Buddha's teachings.
- Violence has never been used to spread Buddhism.
- Buddhism adapts to existing cultures.
- The three main branches of Buddhism are Theravada, Mahayana and Vajrayana.
- A Theravadin Buddhist who has completed the Noble Eightfold Path is called an Arahant.
- Mahayana is a branch or school of Buddhism. Within it there are hundreds of different sects.
- Zen Buddhists try to reveal enlightenment through meditation.
- Tibetan Buddhism is a type of Vajrayana Buddhism.

1 a) Outline the main features of Zen Buddhism. (8 marks)

b) Explain how and why Buddhism spread from India. (8 marks)

c) 'There is no one, single Buddhist faith.'
Do you agree? Give reasons for your answer, showing that you have thought about more than one point of view. (4 marks)

2 a) Describe in detail the similarities and differences between the Theravada, Mahayana and Tibetan schools of Buddhism. (10 marks)

b) Explain why there are different types of Buddhism. (6 marks)

c) 'Buddhism has no relevance in the West.'
Do you agree? Give reasons to support your answer, and show that you have thought about different points of view. (4 marks)

Assignment

The Buddhist Community

3

KEY WORDS

Bhikkhu (Bhikshu – Sanskrit)/Bhikkhuni (Bhikshuni – Sanskrit): A Buddhist monk/nun.

Chorten: A Tibetan stupa.

Dagoba: A Sri Lankan stupa.

Gelong: A Tibetan Buddhist monk.

Lama: A guru, or senior teacher, in Tibetan Buddhism.

Pagoda: A Burmese, Chinese or Japanese stupa.

Patimokkha: Rules for monks and nuns.

Samanera: A novice, or trainee bhikkhu.

Sangha: 'Assembly'. 1. The community of Buddhists; 2. The community of bhikkhus.

Stupa: Monument containing relics of the Buddha or important Buddhist teacher.

Three Refuges: Devotion to the Three Treasures.

Three Treasures (Three Jewels): The Buddha, the Dhamma, the Sangha.

Triple Gem: The Three Treasures.

Vihara: 'Resting Place', a Buddhist monastery.

Wat: A Thai Buddhist temple.

WHAT IS THE SANGHA?

KEY QUESTION

What is the relationship between Buddhist monks and nuns and householder Buddhists?

The word **Sangha** means 'assembly' – a group of people. It is used to describe all those who follow the Buddha and his teachings (Dhamma). In the Theravada tradition Sangha refers to the order of Buddhist monks and nuns, but more generally it can mean all those who practise Buddhism.

Originally the Buddha and his monks (**bhikkhus**) travelled around, meeting together during the rainy season. They were known as homeless brothers. By living this lifestyle they were able to keep their attachments (tanha) to a minimum, and so work towards arahantship. At the same time there were lay followers: people who followed the Dhamma, but continued to live in families and earn their own livings. The lay community (lay Sangha) supported the community of bhikkhus (monastic Sangha) by providing them with food and clothing, and accommodation during the rainy season. These buildings gradually became permanent monasteries (called **viharas**, literally 'resting places') where the monks lived all year.

Theravada

This tradition survives today, especially in Theravadin countries. Buddhist monks and nuns live in monasteries and are supported by lay believers. It is a form of community teamwork. The lay Sangha supports the monastic Sangha by providing the bhikkhus with alms (food and donations of money). On the other hand, the vihara contributes to the life of the lay community. It acts as a community centre and a school, where bhikkhus not only teach children how to read and write, but also teach adults how to build, farm and dig wells. It has the function of a bank, as lay people may use it to deposit valuable belongings for safekeeping; and sometimes it is a hotel for lay believers to stay in when attending religious festivals.

▲ A Buddhist nun in the temple at the Samye Ling Buddhist monastery in Dumfries and Galloway.

Lay Buddhists are happy to contribute to the upkeep of the vihara and the welfare of the bhikkhus. By making donations with a pure heart, they are able to create good or fortunate kamma for themselves. In addition, it is believed that having a vihara in the district brings benefit to all those who live around it, so lay people feel honoured to be able to support it. For their part, in return for the donations they have been given, the bhikkhus lead lay believers in worship and teach them the Dhamma.

Mahayana

Unlike Theravadin Buddhists, Mahayanists do not believe that becoming a monk or nun gives them a unique opportunity to work towards enlightenment. They claim that, since an enlightened being has a deep understanding of the reality of life, those who live and work in the real world have equal access to buddhahood. So Mahayana monks ('bhikshus') do not cut themselves off from all attachments. Indeed, some are married and have families. Therefore, the monastic Sangha in most Mahayanist countries has a slightly different function from that of the Theravada tradition. The relationship between the monastic and lay communities is still one of mutual dependence: they serve each other. It is the duty of the bhikshus to preserve Buddhist treasures and to make sure that the Buddhist teachings do not become corrupted. They do not travel to teach the Dharma; indeed, in many sects it is the lay believers who teach others about Buddhism.

TASK BOX

Describe the relationship between the monastic and lay Sanghas in Theravada Buddhism.

To do this task, you must consider the ways in which bhikkhus help and support lay people, and how lay people support the vihara.

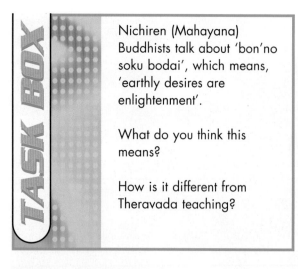

TASK BOX

Nichiren (Mahayana) Buddhists talk about 'bon'no soku bodai', which means, 'earthly desires are enlightenment'.

What do you think this means?

How is it different from Theravada teaching?

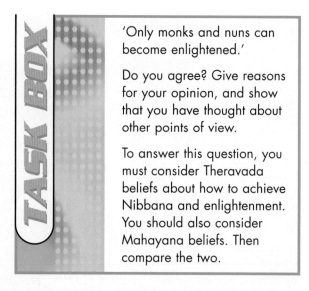

TASK BOX

'Only monks and nuns can become enlightened.'

Do you agree? Give reasons for your opinion, and show that you have thought about other points of view.

To answer this question, you must consider Theravada beliefs about how to achieve Nibbana and enlightenment. You should also consider Mahayana beliefs. Then compare the two.

In Japan especially, some bhikshus are called priests. Those who live and work in monasteries tend not to receive food from lay believers, but eat simply on food grown in the monastery's grounds. Most are, therefore, vegetarian. In addition, they perform domestic chores such as cooking, cleaning and laundry.

Some priests run temples in towns and cities in rather the same way as a Church of England parish priest may in Britain. They conduct certain ceremonies for the lay believers, such as weddings, funerals and memorial services. In return, the lay believers make donations to their local temple.

Tibetan

Until the middle of the twentieth century, the religious life of Tibet was dominated by huge monasteries. It was estimated that one in three of all men became monks, and up to one-fifth of the entire population lived in monasteries. The capital city, Lhasa, had a population of only 20,000, but around it were monasteries with another 20,000 monks living in them.

There are different sects within the Tibetan monastic Sangha. The oldest of these is the Nyingmapa (Red Hats), named after their ceremonial headgear. The Gelugpa (Yellow Hats), a reformed group set up in the fourteenth century, is the largest sect today.

Young boys may become monks. They take temporary vows and are educated in the monastery. As well as reading, writing and maths, they also study Tibetan Buddhist philosophy and scriptures. Most Tibetan men have therefore had at least some experience of monastic life.

Fully ordained monks are called **gelongs**, and senior teachers are called **lamas**. Some of them are married. In most other respects they follow the same traditions as those of other branches of Buddhism, but they do not go out of their monasteries (which are called lamaseries) to receive offerings from lay people.

There are four types of Tibetan monks, and each has a different function:

- Some are students of the Dharma. They are working towards high qualifications and are seen as scholars.
- Some are trained to perform religious ceremonies for the safety and happiness of lay believers.
- Some are specialist craftsmen, such as painters, sculptors, printers or doctors.
- Most monks perform general chores around the monastery.

▲ The Potala Palace at Lhasa.

TEST YOURSELF

1 Which school of Buddhism distinguishes between the monastic and lay Sanghas?
2 What is the difference between the monastic and lay Sanghas?
3 What is the function of Mahayana bhikshus?
4 Which is the largest sect of the Tibetan Sangha?

WHY BECOME A BUDDHIST MONK?

> KEY QUESTION
>
> What is it like to be a Buddhist monk?

In traditional Theravadin countries, it is considered more important for males to be educated than females. It is the men who work to support their families, while women have the responsibility of managing the home. In rural communities, viharas take on the function of schools. They provide an education for boys and men. This means that, if a person wants an education, he must become a bhikkhu. This need not be forever: he may be a bhikkhu for a few years, a few months, or even a few weeks. (In other Buddhist traditions being a bhikkhu is a life-long commitment.)

Joining the Sangha is, however, primarily a religious matter. A person may request ordination into the Sangha because he or she wishes to use the opportunity to work towards Nibbana. A bhikkhu is cut off from all attachments: he has no possessions, no money, no wife or partner, no children. It is therefore easier for him to overcome the cravings that lead to dukkha than for a layperson. A bhikkhu may not go out to work, and so devotes his time to worship, meditation, studying and teaching the Dhamma. In this way he can perfectly focus on becoming an Arahant.

As a bhikkhu, a person has a greater opportunity to learn about the Dhamma. He is then able to teach the Dhamma to others. Buddhists believe that studying and telling others about the Dhamma brings merit, or fortunate kamma. Merit is also gained by the bhikkhu's family.

Ordination ceremonies are slightly different in different Buddhist traditions and different countries. The ceremony we shall look at comes from the Theravada school of Thailand.

▼ The ordination of Thai boys.

◀ An ordinand has his head shaved.

◀ Boys are robed as part of the ordination ceremony.

◀ Studying is an important part of being a bhikkhu.

Before a person takes full ordination and becomes a bhikkhu, he must first be ordained as a **samanera**, or novice (trainee). A person who is about to be ordained is called an ordinand. You can become a samanera at any age, but you cannot become a bhikkhu until you are at least 20. It is very rare for girls and women to become samaneras, and still rarer for them to be fully ordained **bhikkhunis** (nuns). The tradition died out in the 10th century, and is only now beginning to be re-introduced. (See page 139.) In Thailand there are between 80 and 100 thousand samaneras, and 200 to 300 thousand bhikkhus. The numbers change, of course, because some people do not stay as monks for very long.

On the morning of the ceremony, the ordinands' families provide a meal for the bhikkhus of the vihara their sons will join. Young boys are dressed up as the young Prince Siddattha and led on horseback around the vihara. They then have their hair and eyebrows shaved. Members of their families cut bits off first, and then bhikkhus shave their heads completely. This is a symbol of poverty: the fact that they have given up attachments to material things.

'It is selfish to become a Buddhist monk.'

Do you agree? Give reasons to support your answer, and show that you have thought about different points of view.

TASK BOX

The ceremony itself takes place in a special ordination building called a bot. Each ordinand has formally to ask a senior bhikkhu to give him the white robes of a samanera and ordain him. He then 'takes refuge in the **Three Treasures**' and undertakes the Ten Precepts. (The Three Treasures and the Ten Precepts are explained later in this Unit.) At this point, the senior monk promises that he will be the samanera's preceptor, that is, he will act as a mentor and train the novice for full ordination and beyond.

When a samanera becomes a bhikkhu, he attends a ceremony of higher ordination. At this ceremony he is given the saffron-yellow robes of a bhikkhu to wear and an alms bowl for his food. He has to declare that he is healthy, unmarried, free from debt, and that he has his parents' permission to be ordained. The ordinand's preceptor then asks the Sangha to admit the new bhikkhu, and, if no one objects, he receives full ordination.

TEST YOURSELF

1 What reasons might a Theravadin Buddhist have for becoming a bhikkhu?
2 What is ordination?
3 What is a samanera?
4 What happens at a Theravadin ordination ceremony?

▲ A Buddhist monk praying.

WHAT IS LIFE LIKE FOR A BHIKKHU?

Life in a vihara offers a balance between meditation, study and work. It is designed to create the best possible conditions for a person to make spiritual progress. So a Theravadin monk is able to live the Middle Way by possessing only those things that are necessary to support life without causing craving. They are:

- An alms bowl   The word 'bhikkhu' means 'one who shares'. Since the bhikkhu is allowed to earn no money, he must receive his food from lay people who are prepared to provide it. This is not begging on the part of the monk; it is sharing on behalf of the layperson. Lay believers are grateful for the opportunity to do this, because it enables them to show their respect for the bhikkhus, and it gains them merit.
- A razor   This enables the bhikkhu to keep his face and head clean of hair.
- A water strainer   Since a bhikkhu will not knowingly destroy life, he strains drinking water to remove living things that may be in it.
- A needle   This symbolises the bhikkhu's poverty. If his robes tear, he must repair them.

In the 29,000 viharas that function in Thailand, the daily routine followed by the bhikkhus is similar:

4.00 a.m.:	Get up. The monks then meditate for one hour and chant for one hour.
6.00 a.m.:	Alms round. The monks walk around the neighbourhood with their alms bowls. Local lay people put food into their bowls.
7.00 a.m.:	On returning to the monastery, the monks have breakfast together and plan their duties for the day.
8.00 a.m.:	The bhikkhus start work maintaining the vihara.

10.30 a.m.:	Some monks will have lunch at this time. This will be their last meal of the day, as the Ten Precepts do not allow them to eat after midday.
1.00 p.m.:	Classes in the Buddhist Dhamma begin.
5.00 p.m.:	This is a rest period.
6.00 p.m.:	An hour of meditation is followed by an hour of puja (worship) and a talk from a senior bhikkhu.
8.00 p.m.:	Bhikkhus do their homework and private study.
10.00 p.m.:	Bed time.

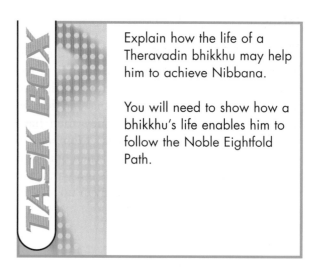

TASK BOX

Explain how the life of a Theravadin bhikkhu may help him to achieve Nibbana.

You will need to show how a bhikkhu's life enables him to follow the Noble Eightfold Path.

In a Tibetan monastery, daily life follows pretty much the same pattern. There is a great emphasis on education and learning. Newly ordained monks learn the Tibetan language and grammar from tantric texts. They are also taught Buddhist philosophy, astrology and medicine. They demonstrate their achievements in public examinations. These take the form of debates between the students and their teachers (lamas). A young monk will have to study for up to 20 years before he can become a Tantric Master.

WHAT CODES OF CONDUCT DO THE BHIKKHUS FOLLOW?

When a bhikkhu is ordained he undertakes the Ten Precepts. The Ten Precepts are not rules. They are really promises that the bhikkhu makes to himself, ideals he wants to live up to. The first five are the Five Precepts that make up Right Action in the Noble Eightfold Path. All Buddhists try to follow them. They are:

1. not to destroy life
2. not to take what is not freely given
3. not to misuse sex
4. not to lie
5. not to cloud the mind with alcohol or drugs.

(These are explained in Unit Seven.)

The other five Precepts are specific to the monastic Sangha, though some lay Buddhists may choose to follow them at certain times of the year. They are:

6. To refrain from eating after midday.
   Human beings need to eat in order to live, but a bhikkhu whose mind is occupied with thoughts of supper is craving, and so is making very slow progress towards buddhahood.
7. To refrain from dancing, singing and watching unsuitable entertainments.
   Enjoyment of such things increases worldly attachment. Bhikkhus are not against entertainment, and would not wish to stop anyone else from enjoying such things. It is their personal decision to avoid them.
8. To refrain from using scents or garlands.
   The Dhamma is life itself. You cannot improve life by making it smell better!
9. To refrain from sleeping on a high or broad (in other words, luxurious) bed.
   A bhikkhu should not think of sleep as an enjoyable pastime, but as a necessity. He can become enlightened only when awake and alert. Most bhikkhus sleep on a thin mat which they roll up during the day to carry with them.
10. To refrain from handling gold and silver (including money).
    A bhikkhu should not be attached to worldly things.

Monks are celibate; in other words, they live without sex. This is because sex can be the most powerful of human cravings and is incompatible with the sort of life that monks have chosen to lead. So, although the third Precept is not to misuse sex, monks and nuns undertake to practise celibacy: 'brahmacharya'. This word means 'to live like the gods' – in other words, to be free from thinking of yourself as either a man or a woman, and to relate to other people without allowing sex to get in the way.

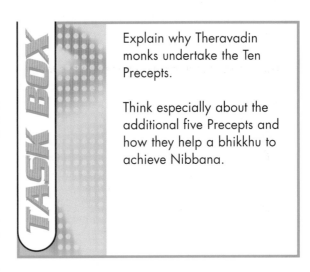

TASK BOX

Explain why Theravadin monks undertake the Ten Precepts.

Think especially about the additional five Precepts and how they help a bhikkhu to achieve Nibbana.

In addition to the Ten Precepts, bhikkhus also undertake 227 **Patimokkha**. The word 'Patimokkha' literally means 'tight bond', and so this is a set of rules that bind the Sangha together. It is hard to imagine a community of people who live together not having any rules. The first rules for bhikkhus were laid down in the time of Siddattha, and developed after that as new rules became necessary. They were written down in an important collection of books known as the Vinaya.

The Buddha himself explained why the rules were necessary. He said that:

- They are for the good of the Sangha.
- They control the monks' behaviour.
- They prevent bad habits developing.
- They increase faith.
- They are part of the Dhamma.

A young Thai boy explains why he became a samanera:

'When my Grandfather died, I was ordained as a samanera. Thai people believe that, when they die, they will go to paradise by holding onto a monk's robe. So I became a monk so that my Grandfather could go to paradise. My Grandfather was cremated about seven days later. Most boys, like my younger brother, become monks only for a day or two. But I was a samanera for a month, because it was the school holidays.

'When I first heard I was to become a monk, I felt a little scared. But later I felt happier about it, though I had to learn a lot of things, like the Ten Precepts. I had to learn them in Pali, which was hard, because it is a very old language and difficult to say. Older monks have to learn and keep 227 rules as well.

'On the first day, the monks woke me up at 5 a.m. They told me to have a bath and put on my robes. Then we had to meditate for half an hour. This was hard, because I had never done it before, so they had to show me what to do.

'At 6 o'clock we left to go on the alms round. We stopped many times for people to give us food and drink. They stood outside their houses and called us over. We were not allowed to say, "Thank you," but we gave them a blessing. When we got back, we picked out the food we wanted to eat.

'After that I played video games, watched TV or listened to the radio. Some mornings I would go out to the shop and buy a snack or a comic book. Other times, my parents would come and visit me. They would bring food, and we would eat it at about 11.30. I wasn't allowed out in the afternoon.

'In the evening we had to meditate again for about 30 minutes. I didn't like meditating, because it was very boring and uncomfortable sitting on the ground. I then went to bed straight away, because I had to get up early in the morning.

'On the last day, my parents came to pick me up. We had a special ceremony. I had to repeat the same Pali words like before to the monks. I also had to change my robes and put my ordinary clothes back on. I was happy to leave, because now I could eat after lunch.

'I didn't enjoy myself being a monk, but I was happy that I could help my Grandfather.'

Nattawud Daoruang, aged 13

Use Nattawud's account to discuss the ordination of boys.

Was his experience as you imagined it might be? What was the same? What was different?

Why did his parents want him to become ordained?

How would you have felt about being ordained if you believed it would help someone you loved?

Why might it be unfair to compare your lifestyle with Nattawud's?

TEST YOURSELF

1 Why do Theravadin bhikkhus have so few possessions?
2 Why do Theravadin bhikkhus undertake five extra Precepts?
3 What are the Patimokkha?
4 Why are the Patimokkha important in the monastic Sangha?

WHAT ARE THE THREE REFUGES?

KEY QUESTION

What does 'faith' mean for a Buddhist?

Everybody experiences degrees of insecurity at all stages of life. A baby depends entirely on its parents for food, warmth and love. As we grow older, and depend on our parents less, we seek the trust of friends and lovers. When things go wrong, we need to feel confidence in someone who is wiser than we are. Most people have sets of beliefs that guide them through life, beliefs that may or may not form a religious faith.

A Buddhist is someone who places his or her trust in the Three Jewels, or the Three Treasures. They are, by definition, things that are precious and hold great value. They are the Buddha, the Dhamma and the Sangha. They are also known as the **Triple Gem**.

The Buddha

Although Buddhists do not worship the Buddha in the sense that people of other faiths worship God, he provides them with the perfect example of the enlightened life. Buddhists can learn from his example and put his wisdom into practice in their daily lives. He is the teacher of all that is important for them.

The Dhamma

The teachings of the Buddha provide Buddhists with a view of life and an outlook that they believe will lead them to perfect happiness. The Dhamma also gives them the means to achieve it. And, while Dhamma means the teachings of the Buddha about the true nature of life, it also refers to the truth about life itself. Dhamma is the law of life. Buddhists believe that, by taking refuge in it, the Dhamma will protect them in their own lives.

The Sangha

The community of Buddhists provides support for each member of it. Buddhists look to other Buddhists for inspiration in their progress towards enlightenment, and seek guidance from them at critical times.

The Three Refuges

Devotion to the Three Treasures is often referred to as the **Three Refuges**. A refuge is a place we go to, or a person we turn to, for safety. For a Buddhist, the world is an insecure place. It is Samsara, the world of dukkha, where everything is subject to change (anicca). The Buddhist therefore seeks refuge in the Buddha, the Dhamma and the Sangha: the teacher, the teaching and the taught. They are sometimes likened to the three legs of a stool. The stool cannot stay upright if one of them is not there: it relies on all three for stability. In the same way, the Three Treasures are interdependent, and Buddhists seek refuge in them.

When a bhikkhu is ordained he confirms his faith in the Three Refuges by reciting three times in Pali:

> Buddham saranam gacchami
> Dhammam saranam gacchami
> Sangham saranam gacchami.

This means in English:

> I take refuge in the Buddha
> I take refuge in the Dhamma
> I take refuge in the Sangha.

For Buddhists, reciting the Three Refuges is more than just stating their beliefs. It is a demonstration of:

- Humility towards the Buddha, his teachings and other people.
- Accepting the Three Treasures as a guiding principle in life.
- Commitment to the Buddhist faith.
- Honouring the Three Treasures.

TASK BOX

Why might the Three Refuges be particularly important for lay Buddhists?

To answer this you will need to think about the nature of dukkha, the insecurity of anicca, and ways in which people form attachments.

TEST YOURSELF

1. What are the Three Treasures?
2. Why are they called 'Treasures'?
3. Why are the Three Treasures also known as 'Refuges'?
4. Why are the Three Refuges important for Buddhists?

WHAT DOES A BUDDHIST MONASTERY LOOK LIKE?

KEY QUESTION

What are Buddhist places of worship like?

After the Buddha died, his body was cremated. His remains were divided up and presented to the various rulers of the tribes and kingdoms of India. These rulers built monuments over the remains called **stupas**. This has remained a tradition in Buddhism, and stupas are still built over the relics of great Buddhist teachers. Although Buddhist viharas and temples vary in design from country to country as well as from school to school, the stupa is a feature that is common to all.

▲ Stupas can be seen behind the figure of the Buddha at this temple.

There is nearly always a path around a stupa which is used for circumambulation. 'Circumambulation' literally means 'walking around'. The paths are often lit up, especially at night, and bhikkhus and lay believers carry incense and lanterns as they make their way around the stupa. This is usually done three times, to represent the Three Treasures. It is a way for a person to make a mindful connection with his or her own buddha nature.

Theravada

The temple–vihara in Thailand is called a **wat**. Nearly every town and village in Thailand has its own wat, which is at the heart of the community. There are nearly 30,000 of them in the country. The main hall of worship is called the wihan. As well as containing a focus of worship, usually a shrine with a statue of the Buddha on it, and sacred texts, there are a great many decorations. There may be, for example, images telling stories of the Buddha's life. It is here that the lay people worship with the bhikkhus, and bring flowers and other gifts to leave at the shrine. The building itself usually faces east, as the Buddha is supposed to have been facing east when he became enlightened.

A stupa in Thailand is known as a chedi. Chedis are traditionally dome-shaped structures containing relics of the Buddha or another important person. On top of the dome is a pole with discs on it. This represents a parasol. It is a symbol of honour, as parasols were used to protect royal personages from the sun in ancient India. At the base of the dome are paths so that worshippers may walk around the stupa. This is a symbol that the Buddha should be at the centre of a person's life, just as his relics are at the centre of the circuit. Many wats have cemeteries attached to them where the ashes of deceased Buddhists are kept under small chedis.

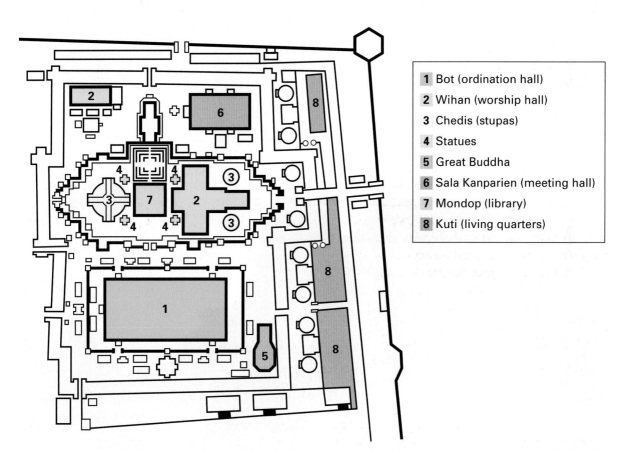

1	Bot (ordination hall)
2	Wihan (worship hall)
3	Chedis (stupas)
4	Statues
5	Great Buddha
6	Sala Kanparien (meeting hall)
7	Mondop (library)
8	Kuti (living quarters)

▲ A plan of a Thai temple.

Also in the temple complex there is a hall used for religious ceremonies such as the ordination of samaneras and bhikkhus, called a bot. Like the wihan, the bot contains a statue of the Buddha and is highly decorated. Precious Buddhist scriptures are stored in a building called a mondop. There is a meeting hall, called a sala kanparien, where the monks conduct the business of the monastery, and kuti, which are the monks' living quarters. Some wats also have a library and a school.

Most temples will also have a bo tree. When Siddattha became enlightened, he was meditating under a pipal (fig) tree. It has since become a symbol of enlightenment, and is known as a bodhi or bo, meaning 'enlightenment', tree. Cuttings were taken from the original tree and some of their descendants are still in existence. In any case, the presence of a bo tree in the temple grounds reminds worshippers of their own capacity to be enlightened.

As in Thailand, Sri Lankan temples contain stupas that house the relics of the Buddha, one of his disciples or an Arahant. They are known as **dagobas**, or 'relic chambers'. The idea of the dagoba crossed the sea to Burma, where the name changed to **pagoda**. Once again, relics of the Buddha or his followers are kept here. They can be large and very ornate structures, decorated in gold leaf, to which lay believers add more leaves out of respect for the Three Treasures – the Buddha, the Dhamma and the Sangha – gaining merit at the same time.

TASK BOX

Explain why Theravadin temples are important for lay Buddhists.

Think about the functions of Theravadin monks, and their relationship with lay believers. Consider, too, ways in which lay believers can gain punna (merit).

▲ A bo tree with two stupas beside it.

Mahayana

Temple complexes in countries where Mahayana is the principal school of Buddhism have a similar layout to Theravadin viharas. The main function of large temples is to house Buddhist treasures, though most towns and cities have small temples that conduct services for local lay people. In Japan, for example, a temple may be a concrete hall on a busy city street, or a large campus in the countryside.

The entrance to a Japanese temple's grounds is usually marked by a gate tower, with several smaller gates on the main pathway through the estate. Each is covered with a sloped and gently curved roof.

The most important building in the complex is the main hall, or hondo, which houses sacred objects, such as statues and Buddhist writings. The hondo is used for grand ceremonies led by the monks, and sometimes attended by lay believers. Minor objects of worship are also kept in halls called kodo. These are principally used for lectures and meetings, but they also contain some of the temple's treasures.

The stupa, which houses remains of the Buddha or great Buddhist teachers, is called a pagoda in Japanese temples. It has evolved from the bell-shaped structure that is still used in Theravadin countries, and incorporates features of classical Japanese design. It has either three or five square storeys, each with its own curved roof. As well as accommodating relics, pagodas sometimes contain photographs and other memorabilia of the deceased.

Also in the temple complex will be accommodation for the priests. In Japan, priests are allowed to marry (and, therefore, cannot properly be called monks), so there is housing for their families. Finally, cemeteries are usually located at temples. Lay people honour their dead ancestors by visiting their graves frequently, especially at anniversaries and festivals.

◄ A Japanese pagoda.

Tibetan

Tibetan Buddhists have stupas, just as in the earlier forms of Buddhism. They are called **chortens**. Like stupas in other traditions, they contain remains of the Buddha, one of his enlightened followers, or great Buddhist teachers of the past. But they are not mere monuments. As with most things in the Buddhist world, they are visual aids, and the clue to one of their meanings for Tibetan Buddhists is given in the fact that they have eyes.

Chortens are made up of five parts or levels that represent various elements, starting with the most solid – earth – at the base, and rising through water, fire and air to pure spirit (or space) at the top. In this way, the Tibetan chorten represents all of reality.

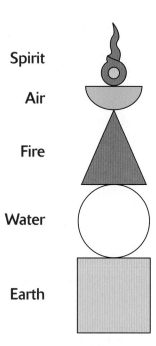

Spirit

Air

Fire

Water

Earth

▲ This decorated chorten has a special symbolic meaning – and the clue is in the eyes!

But these elements in a stupa can also stand for parts of a human being. These are not things you would find physically in the body – they do not appear in books on anatomy! Rather, they are where people tend to express their thoughts and feelings.

- The cube and sphere represent the lower parts of the body, the place where many deep feelings and needs are felt.
- The red cone represents the heart centre, the place from which you experience emotions and make choices. (Feelings of great happiness or sadness may be experienced in the chest.)
- The green inverted hemisphere represents the throat and speech.
- The multicoloured droplet on the top represents the crown of the head and the qualities of enlightenment.

▲ Parts of the human body represented by the elements in the stupa.

So the stupa (or chorten) represents the idea of enlightenment.

At the base of the fire element, chortens have a box, called a harmika. This may contain the remains of the person in whose memory the stupa is built, but it also represents an altar where offerings would be put on a sacred fire. Although the whole stupa represents the Buddha, the harmika represents the point of choice, where a person takes the step towards enlightenment. It has to do with the heart and to do with making offerings. It has eyes: it watches you!

Traditionally, each side of the stupa represents a moment in the life of the Buddha. Some stupas have images to express this.

- East – birth
- South – enlightenment
- West – teaching
- North – death (known as the paraNirvana)

Tibetan Buddhists walk round a stupa in a clockwise direction. That way they follow the life of the Buddha from birth to death.

TEST YOURSELF

1 What is a stupa?
2 Why do Buddhists circumambulate stupas?
3 What is a Thai Buddhist temple called?
4 What is a Japanese stupa known as?

WEBLINKS

* http://www.beyondthenet.
net/sangha/distinctive_marks_
of_the_bhikkhu.htm
*A brief summary of a bhikkhu's
aims.*
* http://www.abm.ndirect.co.uk/
leftside/sumaries/q-a/
on-monlife.htm
*Questions and answers with a
Western Theravadin monk.*
* http://www.orientalarchitecture.
com/bangkok/watphoindex.htm
*A plan and photographs of
Wat Pho, the largest in
Thailand.*
* http://www.foutz.net/japan/
*Photographs of Japanese
temples.*

REMEMBER

▶ For Theravada Buddhists, the word 'Sangha' refers specifically to the monastic Sangha.

▶ For Mahayana Buddhists, 'Sangha' means all who practise the Dharma.

▶ A stupa is a structure built to house relics of the Buddha or an important Buddhist teacher.

▶ Stupas are known by different names in different countries:
Thailand – Chedi
Sri Lanka – Dagoba
Japan – Pagoda
Tibet – Chorten

---

1 a) Give a detailed description of the life of a Theravadin bhikkhu. (8 marks)

b) Explain why temples are important for Buddhists. (7 marks)

c) 'Religious people should earn their own living and not depend on the generosity of others.'
Do you agree? Give reasons for your answer, showing that you have thought about more than
one point of view. (5 marks)

2 a) Describe the main features of a stupa. (6 marks)

b) Explain how Buddhists might show commitment to the Three Refuges. (8 marks)

c) 'Buddhists should visit temples if they want to be enlightened.'
Do you agree? Give reasons for your opinion, showing that you have considered another
point of view. (6 marks)

Assignment

4

KEY WORDS

Kathina: A festival during which lay Buddhists donate robes to the vihara.

Pavarana Day: A day when bhikkhus reflect on their behaviour during the Vassa.

Uposatha Day (Moon Day): The fortnightly recitation of the Patimokkha.

Vassa: The rainy season in South East Asia.

Wesak: A festival to commemorate the birth, enlightenment and death of the Buddha.

WHY DO BUDDHISTS HAVE SPECIAL DAYS?

KEY QUESTION

Why are festivals important to Buddhists?

Unlike some other religions, Buddhism has no special day of the week reserved for worship. All the same, there are days throughout the year that have religious significance. As Buddhism is practised differently in different countries according to local customs and traditions, each of these countries has different festivals. However, there are some festivals that are common to each branch of Buddhism, and, although they may be celebrated slightly differently, they still have much in common.

All Buddhist festivals are times when people can meet and share their joy at the occasion. Lay people visit temples and participate in acts of worship with the monks. Festivals are therefore one way of bringing the Sangha together. They are also a way of making merit, accumulating fortunate kamma and, since they are religious occasions, they provide opportunities for people to reflect on their faith and renew their commitment to it.

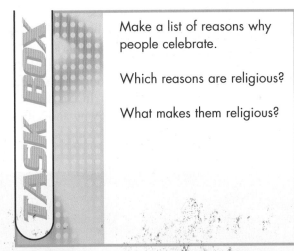

TASK BOX

Make a list of reasons why people celebrate.

Which reasons are religious?

What makes them religious?

▲ Making offerings is an important part of Buddhist worship.

Wesak

Vesakha is the name of the ancient Indian month that roughly corresponds with the month of May in the modern calendar. **Wesak** is the Theravadin festival that takes place on the day of the full moon of that month. It commemorates the birth, enlightenment and death of the Buddha. It is probably the most important and widely celebrated festival in Buddhism.

The coming of an enlightened being to this world is seen as a rare and important event. The Buddha and his teachings can be compared to a light that illuminates the darkness of Samsara. Therefore, light is used as a symbol of all three aspects of the festival: the Buddha's birth, enlightenment and passing away. Festival goers light lanterns, and carry them through the streets and hang them outside houses. In Sri Lanka, there are great processions in towns and cities with brightly lit floats.

TASK BOX

Explain why light is used as a symbol.

Think about the properties of light: its abilities to give illumination and heat, life and death. Think, too, about the ways in which human life is affected by light or its absence. Finally, consider how and why Buddhists use light as a symbol at Wesak, and compare it with the ways in which light is used symbolically in other religious traditions.

▲ Light is used as a symbol during Wesak.

At Wesak, lay believers make a special effort to make donations to the bhikkhus. Some take on the extra five Precepts reserved for bhikkhus in addition to the Five Precepts that they undertake as lay people. So, just for the duration of Wesak, they will also undertake not to eat after midday, not to sleep in a luxurious bed, not to wear jewellery, make-up or scent, not to go to musical entertainment and not to handle money.

Bhikkhus and lay believers will spend the day together in the temple attending lectures on the scriptures, learning about aspects of the Buddha's life, chanting from religious texts and meditating. Stupas are lit up, and so are the paths around them as families walk around them. Stalls are set up to give away food and drink to passers by. Wesak is sometimes called Buddha Day.

Rain retreats

After Siddattha became enlightened, he was reluctant to teach others the Dhamma. He thought that they would not be able to understand it. Tradition has it that a Hindu god persuaded him to go out and preach, and that his first sermon took place in the Deer Park at Sarnath. It was given to the Five Ascetics (see pp. 6 and 74) on the subject of the Middle Way, an event known as 'Setting in Motion the Wheel of the Dhamma'. This was, in effect, the start of Buddhism as a religion.

This first teaching is believed to have been given in the ancient Indian month of Asalha, which is roughly equivalent to July. In the Theravadin Sangha it is commemorated on the day of that month's full moon, known as Dhamma Day, when bhikkhus chant the Buddha's first sermon, the Dhamma Cakka Sutta, in the Pali language.

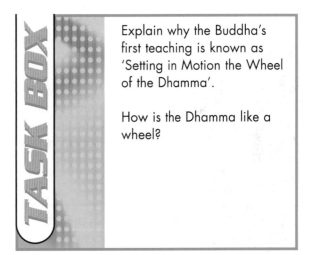

TASK BOX

What reasons might lay Buddhists have for undertaking the five monastic Precepts during Wesak?

TASK BOX

Explain why the Buddha's first teaching is known as 'Setting in Motion the Wheel of the Dhamma'.

How is the Dhamma like a wheel?

TEST YOURSELF

A B C

1 Why do Buddhists celebrate festivals together?
2 What do Buddhists remember at Wesak?

Asalha marks the beginning of the **Vassa**, the three-month rainy season. Viharas were established during the Buddha's lifetime for bhikkhus to stay in during the monsoons. It was seen as an opportunity to reflect, to study and to meditate. The tradition of rain retreats has continued, and today bhikkhus use the Vassa as a time to re-energise their commitment to the Dhamma.

Lay people, too, use the Vassa to advance their spiritual progress. They make determinations to give up old habits like smoking or eating certain foods that form the attachments that slow down their progress. Some lay believers become ordained for the rainy season, returning to their regular lives at the end of it.

There are clearly difficulties involved in sharing the same space as a lot of other people for such a long period of time. Bhikkhus are human and can experience the same strains in relationships as other people. The end of the Vassa is marked by **Pavarana Day** – 'Telling-off Day' – when each bhikkhu invites the rest of the Sangha to reflect on his behaviour during the Rain Retreat. During the ceremony that takes place on that day, the bhikkhus say:

> 'Venerable Ones, I invite reprimand from the Sangha. According to what has been seen, heard or suspected of my actions, may the Venerable Ones correct me out of their compassion. Recognising it is my fault, I shall make amends.'

It should not be seen as a chance for the bhikkhus to 'have a go' at each other, but rather as a recognition of their humanity and an opportunity to 'get things out in the open' and so strengthen relationships.

During the Vassa, the bhikkhus and lay people have had little to do with each other. Now it is over, the bhikkhus will start to move on. Before they do, the lay and monastic communities get together in a festival of unity called **Kathina**. Some families welcome their children home again, and all congratulate the bhikkhus on their retreat, for it is believed that they have created merit for the whole community. On this occasion, lay believers contribute robes and other essential equipment to the vihara. The word 'Kathina' refers to a sewing frame on which the robes used to be made.

Kathina can take place at any time during the month following the Vassa (usually October or November). The lay community provides a meal for the bhikkhus in the morning, and the robes are presented at a ceremony in the afternoon. It is seen as a way of creating great merit for those who are generous enough to contribute.

Uposatha days

Until comparatively recently in human history, calendars were worked out on the basis of the length of time it takes the moon to revolve around the earth. This is called the lunar calendar. (Today, of course, we use the solar calendar, based on the movement of the earth around the sun.) The phases of the moon follow a consistent pattern, so events could be held regularly by timing them to coincide with those phases.

Uposatha Days (sometimes called Moon Days) are held every fortnight, at the new moon and full moon. They are not, strictly speaking, festivals or celebrations, but ceremonies that are held during which the bhikkhus renew their vows to keep the 227 Patimokkha rules of the monastic Sangha.

Uposatha Days are seen as times of renewal, opportunities to purify one's life. On the day before, bhikkhus shave their heads as a symbol of purity. They confess their faults. They clean their bodies thoroughly, and there is a great emphasis on meditation to clarify the mind. The purpose is twofold: first to rid oneself of moral impurity, and second to rid oneself of spiritual ignorance. The idea, then, is to become mindful and awake.

TASK BOX

a) What kinds of problems may occur between bhikkhus during the Vassa?
b) Do you think that a Pavarana Day at the end of the Vassa is a good idea? Give reasons to back up your opinion, and reasons why some people may have a different point of view.
c) Pavarana Day is thought to be beneficial for all the bhikkhus, not just the one confessing his faults. Why do you think this may be so?

▲ Bhikkhus recite the Patimokkha together.

TASK BOX

Explain why bhikkhus believe it is so important to learn and recite the Patimokkha once a fortnight.

Why do you think they recite it together?

PERSPECTIVES

'Since the Dhamma aims at freedom and depends on self-reliance, wouldn't it be better to let the monks develop their own sense of right and wrong unfettered by laws?'

Thanissaro Bhikkhu

What is your opinion? (Remember to give reasons.)

How do you think Thanissaro Bhikkhu would answer his own question?

What do you think would happen if there were no laws in society?

Lay people traditionally join in with the bhikkhus on Uposatha Days. They provide food and eat with them in the morning. Traditionally they dress in white, as a symbol of purity, and some will undertake the Ten Precepts. They will also join in meditation and the meeting in which the bhikkhus recite the Patimokkha.

TEST YOURSELF

1 What do Buddhists do during the Vassa?
2 Why is Pavarana Day important for bhikkhus?
3 How often do Uposatha Days occur?
4 Why are Uposatha Days important for bhikkhus?

a) Explain why Buddhists celebrate festivals.
There are two ways you could answer this question:

Either: Outline the reasons, and then provide examples from features of the festivals;
Or: Describe significant aspects of Buddhist festivals, and highlight reasons why they are important for Buddhists.

b) 'Religious festivals are just an excuse for people to have a good time.'
Do you agree? Give reasons to support your answer, and show that you have thought about different points of view. You must refer to Buddhism in your answer.

WHY ARE PLACES ASSOCIATED WITH THE LIFE OF THE BUDDHA IMPORTANT TO BUDDHISTS?

KEY QUESTION

Which places are special to Buddhists?

For Buddhists, Siddattha Gotama was, first and foremost, a human being: an enlightened being, but human nonetheless. Yet he is considered to be the perfect example of an enlightened being. So Buddhists do not follow him, but the example he set in following the Dhamma. Some Buddhists will therefore try to visit some of the places that are associated with important events in the life of the Buddha. This gives them an opportunity to reflect on what happened at these sites and how they may learn from those happenings.

Journeys made for religious reasons are called pilgrimages, and those who go on them, pilgrims. Buddhist pilgrims may choose to visit the place of Siddattha's birth, the place of his enlightenment, the place of his first teaching, or the place of his death. Some may wish to visit locations associated with other events in the history of their religion, or temples and stupas associated with particular Buddhist teachers.

Pilgrimage is a way of learning more about the Dhamma. It is also a way for Buddhists to devote time to reflecting on themselves, to discovering things about themselves and making progress on their spiritual journey. It shows them that spiritual discovery can come out of earthly experiences. Buddhists believe, too, that undertaking a pilgrimage is a way of gaining merit.

a) Outline the ways in which a pilgrimage is different from a holiday.

b) The Buddha said, 'Ananda (his closest disciple), there are four places the sight of which will arouse strong emotion in those with faith.' 'Which four places?' 'Where the Tathagatha ("Thus Come One" – an honorific title of the Buddha) was born: this is the first. Where the Tathagatha attained enlightenment: this is the second. Where the Tathagatha set in motion the Wheel of the Dhamma: this is the third. Where the Tathagatha attained final Nibbana: this is the fourth. And the monk, the nun, the layman or the laywoman who has faith should visit these places.' *Maha-parinibbana Sutta*

What sorts of 'strong emotion' do you think the Buddha was referring to? Why do you think the Buddha specified these four places for Buddhist pilgrimage?

Lumbini

Lumbini is situated near the border between India and Nepal in the north of the subcontinent. It has a particular significance for Buddhists, because it is the location of Prince Siddattha's birth.

After the birth, Queen Maya, Siddattha's mother, returned with the baby to the palace at nearby Kapilavastu. She died shortly afterwards, and Siddattha remained with the royal household until he was 29 years old, when he left on his quest of spiritual discovery.

Kapilavastu and the surrounding area, including Lumbini, were attacked and left in ruins, even in the Buddha's own lifetime. It is said that, when the Emperor Asoka, the first Buddhist ruler, discovered the place a couple of centuries later, his adviser used magical powers to identify the sites associated with Siddattha's birth. Asoka built a stupa there and erected a pillar to commemorate the event that had taken place.

Again the site fell derelict. Asoka's pillar was destroyed by lightning, and Lumbini was taken over by the surrounding jungle. It was rediscovered at the end of the nineteenth century, and positively identified by an inscription found on a surviving fragment of Asoka's pillar. Today, archaeological remains are still being unearthed at the site.

In 1956, a Theravadin temple was built by Nepalese Buddhists. As well as providing a place for people to worship, it offers retreats and accommodation for pilgrims.

A Tibetan Buddhist monastery was built at Lumbini in 1975. It is a place of safety for Tibetan Buddhist monks who have had to leave their homeland because of the Chinese occupation. They can practise and teach the Dharma in a security that they would not have in Tibet. The monastery itself is very elaborately decorated, and contains lavish murals depicting scenes of Siddattha's nativity.

Bodh Gaya

Bodh Gaya is the place where Siddattha became a buddha. He sat under a pipal (fig) tree and meditated deeply until he was enlightened. The focal point of the site is the Mahabodhi (Great Buddha) Temple. The temple is ancient, though no one knows quite how old it is. It was certainly there in the seventh century CE, and it is likely that it was first built a long time before that. It has been the object of violence and destruction over the centuries, and there have been disputes over who owns it. It was well into the twentieth century that the temple was finally given over to Buddhists.

▲ **The Mahabodhi Temple in Bodh Gaya.**

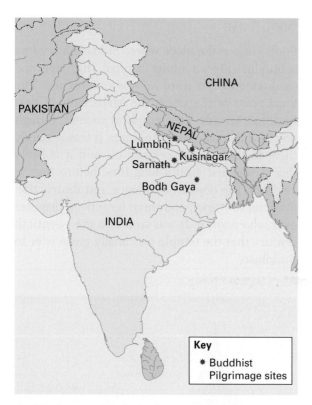

▲ Pilgrimage sites in India.

Sarnath

After his enlightenment, the Buddha left Bodh Gaya for Benares. When he arrived, he went on his alms round, bathed, ate his meal, and then set out to Sarnath. It was there he was to meet again the Five Ascetics who had left him before.

He found them in the Deer Park. They were still trying to find enlightenment through self-denial. When they saw Siddattha, they did not at first recognise his enlightened nature, and ignored him. But as he got closer, the ascetics found themselves drawn to him. They welcomed him as a Buddha.

At first, nothing was said. Then, as the evening grew on, the Buddha began to 'turn the wheel of the Dhamma': he spoke about the Four Noble Truths and the Middle Way to Nibbana. As a result, the Five Ascetics all became Arahants.

The name of the Deer Park comes from a story about one of the Buddha's previous lives. As a deer, he is said to have sacrificed himself for another. The place itself was established as an important religious centre during the Buddha's lifetime. Remains of early monasteries have been uncovered, as has a fragment of the pillar set up by the Emperor Asoka.

Originally two stupas were erected in the Deer Park, though only one remains today. A museum houses much of what has been unearthed at the site. There is a large Theravadin temple that contains relics of the Buddha, and there is a library attached to it that contains important Buddhist scriptures. There is also a Tibetan printing works that has produced a large number of rare texts.

Three stupas mark places associated with events following the Buddha's enlightenment. A key activity that is undertaken around the stupas is circumambulation ('walking around'). We have already seen that this is common practice at stupas in temple complexes.

Worshippers generally walk three times around the stupas, once for each of the Three Treasures. This is not only a way of honouring the Buddha, but it is also a way of drawing out the qualities of buddhahood. It puts them at the centre of one's life.

Temples from many Buddhist sects have been built in the area around Bodh Gaya. They offer retreats and courses in meditation for Buddhists and non Buddhists. Buddhist masters are invited to teach at the temples, and each year thousands of people come from all over the world to hear them.

▲ Dhamekh Stupa in Sarnath.

Kusinagar

When he was in his 81st year, the Buddha decided that he had fulfilled his purpose in the world and that it was time for him to pass away. He ate food knowing that it was bad, forbidding others to eat it. He left the house of his last meal, and walked to the banks of the Hiranyavati River near Kusinagar. There he lay on his side between two tall trees, surrounded by some of his disciples, and told them, 'Everything changes; nothing is constant. Work out your own salvation with diligence.' These were his last words before he died.

The Buddha's body was taken to the river, where it was cremated. His ashes were divided and eventually sent across Asia.

Kusinagar was explored by the great Buddhist Emperor Asoka, who built stupas at the various places where the events leading up to and following the Buddha's death took place. He had a pillar built, inscribed with a description of these events, and a temple that contained a statue of the dying Buddha.

TASK BOX

What do you think the Buddha meant by his last words?

In order to answer this question, you should first consider Buddhist ideas about impermanence, and also what the word 'salvation' may mean in Buddhism.

It appears that there was a thriving monastic community at Kusinagar until the decline of Buddhism in India. The remains were found towards the end of the nineteenth century. They now surround a modern shrine, which contains a huge figure of the dying Buddha dating from the fifth century CE.

▲ A detail of the Buddha's death.

Behind the shrine is a stupa, and the temple marking the Buddha's final resting place has been restored. A large stupa stands at the place of his cremation. Other temples include a Burmese temple in the Theravada tradition, a Tibetan temple, and a Chinese temple that has been converted into an international meditation centre.

TEST YOURSELF

A
B
C

1 Why do Buddhists make pilgrimages?
2 How did the Emperor Asoka mark places associated with the life of the Buddha?
3 What do Buddhists do on pilgrimage?
4 Why did Buddhist pilgrimage sites remain largely undiscovered until the nineteenth century?

TASK BOX

Design a brochure for British Buddhist pilgrims in India.

Remember, this is not a holiday brochure. You should describe the sites associated with the life of the Buddha, why they are significant, and what activities pilgrims can undertake at each site. Click on the images link at http://www.google.co.uk/ to search for pictures with which to illustrate your brochure.

REMEMBER

▶ Buddhists make pilgrimages to famous temples or places associated with important Buddhist teachers, not just the Buddha.

▶ Buddhists do not have a special day of the week for worship.

▶ Different Buddhist countries and traditions celebrate festivals in different ways.

▶ The main pilgrimage sites for Buddhists are those associated with the Buddha's birth, enlightenment, first teaching and death.

▶ There are no Buddhist ceremonies to mark birth or marriage.

▶ Buddhists celebrate festivals at home as well as in temples.

▶ Uposatha days are opportunities for bhikkhus to renew their commitment to the Patimokkha rules.

---

1 a) Describe in detail the meanings of two Buddhist festivals, and how they are celebrated. (8 marks)

   b) Explain the importance of visiting places associated with the life of the Buddha for some Buddhists. (7 marks)

   c) 'You don't have to follow the Buddha to be Buddhist.'
   Do you agree? Give reasons for your opinion, showing that you have considered another point of view. (5 marks)

2 a) Describe a pilgrimage to sites associated with the life of the Buddha. (10 marks)

   b) Explain why bhikkhus observe Uposatha days. (5 marks)

   c) 'Pilgrimage is not an important feature of Buddhism.'
   Do you agree? Give reasons to support your answer and show that you have thought about different points of view. (5 marks)

Assignment

5

KEY WORDS

Anapanasati: 'Mindfulness of the breath' in samatha.

Bhavana: 'Cultivation' or meditation.

Brahma viharas: The four sublime states: compassion, loving kindness, sympathetic joy for others, and even-mindedness.

Dhyana: 'Meditation'.

Kasina: An object of focus in meditation.

Lhagtong: Vipassana in Tibetan Buddhism.

Mala: A string of beads used as an aid to mindfulness in puja.

Mandala: A pattern created to represent spiritual reality.

Mantra: A phrase chanted repeatedly during worship to evoke particular aspects of enlightenment.

Mudra: Symbolic hand gestures used in Tibetan worship or on Buddha rupas.

Puja: Worship.

Rupa: 'Form', an image of the Buddha.

Samatha: Meditation to establish calmness.

Thanka: In Tibetan Buddhism, a wall-hanging depicting the Buddha or an aspect of Buddhism.

Vajra: 'Thunderbolt', a symbol of power in Tibetan Buddhism.

Vipassana: 'Insight', meditation to see clearly the true nature of things.

Zhiney: Samatha in Tibetan Buddhism.

WHAT IS PUJA?

> ### KEY QUESTION
> What does worship mean for Buddhists?

Puja is the word that some Buddhists use for 'worship'. Worship is the expression of devotion, respect, admiration and love for something. People 'worship' all sorts of things: money, celebrity, football, fashion. It is a mixture of emotions and actions that give worth to something, that show its value.

In a sense, worship is a form of exercise. Just as people exercise their bodies by working out, or jogging, or playing squash, so worship is a way of exercising your spiritual side. It is a means of gaining access to your emotions, your deepest thoughts and feelings, your true nature.

Puja, then, involves honouring something by giving it devoted attention. In most religions, the object of worship is God. Believers worship God either directly, or through other respected figures, like saints in the case of Christianity. For Buddhists, puja means investigating the true nature of life in order to reveal enlightenment.

There are three aspects to Buddhist puja:

1. Looking inwards The first step is to look in oneself for those qualities that are worthy of respect, love and admiration. These will be positive characteristics.
2. Development Next, the worshipper will want to develop those qualities, to make them stronger and bring them to the surface.
3. Extension Here the idea is to spread these positive feelings so that they reach all beings.

It is natural for humans to express their emotions physically. Music is one way of doing it: the feelings expressed through a ballad are likely to be very different to those that come through in a piece of thrash metal! The kinds of positive feelings Buddhists try to develop and spread are emotions like love, compassion, kindness, peace and freedom. They do this through various activities and rituals that involve movement, sound, colour and artefacts (objects).

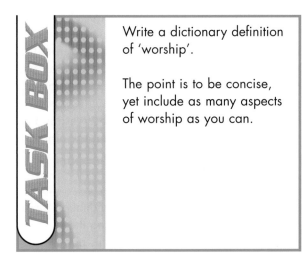

Write a dictionary definition of 'worship'.

The point is to be concise, yet include as many aspects of worship as you can.

How do Buddhists worship?

It is important to understand that most Buddhists do not worship the Buddha, even if they are facing a statue of him when they are practising puja. They reflect on the qualities of the Buddha, and try to develop these qualities in themselves for the benefit of all beings.

Puja is a way of involving the emotions in following the Buddhist path. Celebrating, saying 'Thank you', confessing faults, wishing someone well – Buddhist puja allows a person to do all these things in a simple and direct way. It does not work by magic, but it allows a person's emotions to come into harmony with their thoughts and actions.

There are no rules about how long or how often one should worship. Some lay Buddhists find it helpful to have a shrine at home and to perform simple acts of worship each day. Others go to a temple to worship – some daily, some only at special festivals. Wherever it takes place, the act of puja will generally consist of two elements: meditation and chanting.

TEST YOURSELF

1 What does 'puja' mean?
2 What are the aims of puja?
3 What sorts of emotions are involved in puja?
4 What sorts of activities are involved in puja?

HOW DO BUDDHISTS MEDITATE?

KEY QUESTION
Why do Buddhists meditate?

Buddhists would say that, for most of the time, we are living in a state of delusion: we are fooling ourselves. We imagine that we would be perfectly and permanently happy if only we won the lottery, if only we could lose weight, if only we had a steady relationship, if only ... We kid ourselves into thinking that things we know will change (anicca) will stay the same; that our cravings for things (tanha) will make us happy; that the things that cause us pain (dukkha) are sources of pleasure; that things are what they seem to be, when in reality they are not (anatta). A Buddhist would say that this is unrealistic: it is not seeing life as it really is.

The purpose of Buddhist meditation, then, is to see life clearly, as it really is. This means to look deeply into oneself, freeing oneself from delusion, ending ignorance and craving, and revealing peace and wisdom. Meditation in Buddhism is usually called **dhyana** (Sanskrit) or jhana (Pali). Sometimes it is called **bhavana**, which means 'cultivation' or 'self-development'.

The problem is, when we start to look into ourselves, we cannot find what we are looking for. Our minds are constantly filled with thoughts, jumbled with ideas, and we flit from one idea to another. If we want to focus our thoughts, we need first to clear our minds of the clutter that fills them. Then we are able to examine what it is we want to focus on without being distracted. We need a technique to enable us to concentrate, and then, once we have cleared a space, a means to examine and get to understand the focus of our concentration.

In Buddhism, the technique of mental concentration is called **samatha**, and the means to gain insight is called **vipassana**.

SAMATHA

If you want to find something in a full and untidy cupboard, it is sometimes helpful to empty the cupboard first: to clear it out completely, get rid of the unwanted stuff, and then you will be able to see what you are looking for. When you do this with your mind it is called samatha. The word 'samatha' has a range of meanings, but our word 'concentration' covers all of them. You do not have to be a Buddhist to practise samatha, but Buddhists use it to clear the mind of clutter.

The idea of samatha is to choose something on which to focus the mind, something simple to start with. The mind wanders off it, but you should gently try to bring it back to the subject again; and as the mind wanders again, you should keep trying to refocus.

This kind of concentration is a skill, like riding a bicycle or playing a musical instrument. The more you do it, the better you become at it. And the better you become, the more easily you are able to tackle more complicated exercises. Someone who is well practised in samatha will choose complex ideas to focus on. An angry person may focus on the idea of peace; a greedy person may choose generosity.

A commonly used method of concentration, particularly for beginners, is known as **anapanasati**, breathing meditation. Here breathing itself is the object of concentration. The first stage is to sit in a comfortable position. Buddhists usually sit in the lotus position: cross-legged with each foot resting, sole up, on the opposite thigh. This may be rather difficult to start with, so simply sitting cross-legged on the floor, or in an upright chair is

fine. The back should be straight, and the body in such a position that it will not get restless. The idea is to fix the mind on the point at which breath leaves the nostrils. Breathing should not be forced, but natural. To start with, you could count the breaths, both in and out, to keep the mind focused, but after a while this should not be necessary. Note the breath as it enters and leaves the body, and observe the movement of the body as it happens. In time, breathing will become more delicate, and it may even appear to stop altogether. There is no thought involved, simply observation. It is the observation that should fill the mind: remember that the object of the exercise is mindfulness.

Another focus of samatha that is often used is walking. Like breathing, it is something we all do, it comes easily to us, and generally we do it without thinking. But again, the idea is to become more mindful, to become better at samatha, not better at walking!

For this exercise, you should choose a piece of ground where you can walk in a circle, or to and fro in a straight line, without any obstacles. Start to walk naturally, counting the steps, if this makes it easier for you to concentrate. As you walk, become aware of the movement of your body, feel the ground beneath your feet and the air through which you pass. Let your mind settle into the whole experience of walking.

▲ Walking meditation.

Samatha, then, means paying attention to the movements of the body and the changing states of the mind in order to discover their real nature. The important thing is not to associate them with yourself, because there is no self to associate them with (anatta). Observe them objectively, as things in themselves.

An object that is used as a focus in samatha is called **kasina**. It could be almost anything: a coloured disc, a stone, a tree, a candle flame. Concentration on it should become so focused that you can see the kasina as clearly with the eyes shut as with them open. This is what mindfulness is: complete concentration. At this point, sense activity ceases: all there is is mindfulness.

The brahma viharas

Brahma vihara means 'sublime (or excellent) state'. The brahma viharas are considered to be the ideal qualities for a person to develop, the highest emotions, the things that promote harmony between people. We have seen that the word 'vihara' means 'resting place'. So, the four qualities should be states of mind in which we feel at home. The brahma viharas are used by some Buddhists as objects of concentration, and can be used for deeper meditation. They are:

- Metta (love) In meditating upon metta, a person tries to develop loving kindness in him or herself, and then spread it out to all beings.
- Karuna (compassion) This is the active state of love in which a person is able to understand and share the suffering of others.
- Mudita (sympathetic joy) In this state, the meditator shares the happiness of all other beings.
- Uppekha (equanimity) This is a state of peace and serenity in which a person looks on all other beings with the same positive attitude of care and well-wishing.

TASK BOX

Try reciting the following, slowly and clearly.

'I will abide pervading one quarter with a mind imbued with loving kindness (or compassion or gladness or equanimity). Likewise the second, likewise the third, likewise the fourth; so above and below, around and everywhere and to all as to myself. I will abide pervading the all-encompassing world with a mind imbued with loving kindness (or compassion or gladness or equanimity) abundant, exalted, immeasurable, without hostility and without ill-will.'

Although the words may be difficult to understand, use your knowledge of brahma vihara bhavana to try to explain them.

Meditating on the brahma viharas

A person who has cultivated the brahma viharas is unable to hate or experience feelings of prejudice or anger. For Buddhists, then, it is important not just to try to be guided by the brahma viharas, but to meditate on them in order to draw on and develop the qualities inside oneself. This form of meditation is known as brahma vihara bhavana.

When meditating on the brahma viharas, and spreading them to all beings, you should start with the easiest and move gradually to the more difficult. In metta bhavana (meditation on love), for example, one starts with wishes for one's own happiness: 'May I be free from ill-will; may I be free from suffering; may I be happy.' This is used as a base from which to spread the same wish to others. First, you may think of loved ones, friends or family, and make the same wish to them: 'May they be free from ill-will; may they be free from suffering; may they be happy.' Then the wish can be extended to acquaintances (people you know a little), and to enemies, and to all beings. Then you can break down the barriers between these groups, so that your metta is communicated to your enemies as sincerely as it is to your loved ones.

The aim of metta bhavana is to embed metta firmly in the mind so that it drives all thoughts words and deeds spontaneously.

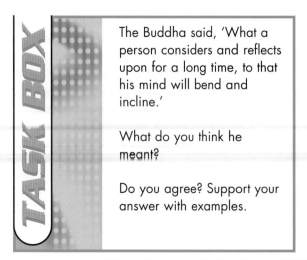

The Buddha said, 'What a person considers and reflects upon for a long time, to that his mind will bend and incline.'

What do you think he meant?

Do you agree? Support your answer with examples.

VIPASSANA

Vipassana means 'insight'. Insight is the ability to see things clearly, to get to the heart of things. It means to recognise the truth of something, often suddenly, in a flash.

It is rather like 'getting' the punch line of a joke. With some jokes, some people get it and some do not. Some do not at first, and then out of the blue it dawns on them. It is like suddenly understanding something, maybe a mathematical principle, that baffled you before. Or seeing the image in a magic-eye picture.

Vipassana means having insight into the nature of life. The nature of life, as we have seen, is described as Three Universal Truths – anicca, anatta, dukkha – impermanence, non-self and suffering. It is one thing to read about these things and understand the logic of them. It is another thing to actually feel the truth of them.

Vipassana meditation is the means to gain this insight. It is a technique that cannot be learned from a book: it must be taught by a master. Only one who is skilled in it can pass it on to pupils. Samatha is sometimes used as a preparation for vipassana. Samatha is not, strictly speaking, a meditative practice: it is a system of concentrating the mind. But it paves the way for deep meditation: vipassana. Someone may practise samatha to overcome attachments, and then practise vipassana to develop the wisdom that comes from overcoming attachments.

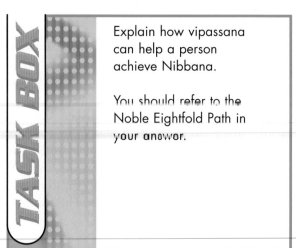

Explain how vipassana can help a person achieve Nibbana.

You should refer to the Noble Eightfold Path in your answer.

Vipassana is usually practised in a sitting position, with legs crossed and the feet resting, soles upward, on the thighs. The back should be perfectly straight, at 90 degrees to the legs. This is known as the lotus position. However, someone who is well practised in vipassana can do it while sitting, walking, standing or lying down.

TEST YOURSELF

1. What is the purpose of meditation?
2. Describe two ways of practising samatha.
3. What are the brahma viharas?
4. What is vipassana?
5. Why is samatha a good preparation for vipassana?

Meditation is conducted with the back straight and eyes half shut, looking downwards but not focused on anything. This prevents you from becoming drowsy or fidgety. In a Japanese Zen meditation hall (zendo), there is a priest who walks around with a stick. If you start to feel sleepy, or tense across the shoulders, he will hit you with the stick to keep you alert.

Vajrayana meditation

Tibetan Buddhists follow the same patterns of meditation as other Buddhists. They use samatha (which they call **zhiney**) to detach themselves from the world of Samsara, realise selflessness (anatta), and develop compassion (karuna) for all living beings. This prepares them for insight meditation, which they call **lhagtong** meditation.

Those who practise Tantric Buddhism use visualisation in their meditation. This means not only reflecting on a certain subject or idea, but also using the imagination to become that thing. For example, meditation on a Buddha may involve visualising oneself as that Buddha. Meditation on death may involve imagining oneself to be dead.

Sometimes Tibetan Buddhists will use objects to help them in their visualisation and meditation. They may meditate over the bones of a deceased lama, for instance, to help them grasp the ideas of impermanence (anicca) and selflessness (anatta). They also use pictures on wall-hangings, called **thankas**, to focus their attention and bring about mindfulness. The wheel of life (see p. 25), for example, may be represented as a thanka. **Mandalas** are circular designs that show various aspects of buddhahood, and they, too, are popular subjects for thankas. Sometimes mandalas are made of brightly coloured sands laid out into a pattern on a board. They may take many weeks to complete. When they are finished, they are not left to be admired as pieces of art. The sand is brushed away. They are used as an aid to mindfulness about the impermanent nature of life (anicca).

TEST YOURSELF

1. What is zhiney?
2. What is Tantric visualisation?
3. What is a thanka?
4. What is a mandala?

WHY DO BUDDHISTS CHANT?

KEY QUESTION

How else do Buddhists worship?

In the time of the Buddha, and for a few centuries afterwards, it was common practice to memorise important teachings, and not write them down. Writing down great teachings was thought to make them vulgar, so the Buddha's teachings were passed on by word of mouth. When the early bhikkhus wanted to agree on the exact words of a teaching, they would recite them together. This could not work if everyone simply spoke the teaching, because everyone talks at different speeds and emphasises different words. So the teachings were chanted.

Chanting is a bit like singing on one note. In order to do it properly, you should hum deeply through the nose and say the phrase at the same time. Chanting has a definite pace and rhythm, so everyone recites the same thing at the same time.

What do Buddhists chant?

The teachings that are chanted are usually in a foreign and ancient language: it could be Pali, Sanskrit or classical Chinese. This does not mean that you have to learn that language, or even understand the meaning of what you are reciting. Over time, however, Buddhists find it helpful to learn the meaning of the texts they chant, and to learn the texts by heart so that they do not have to read them. The learning in itself is often found to be beneficial: it encourages patience, concentration, effort and determination.

Most Buddhist ceremonies have some chanting in them: acts of puja (both in a temple and at home), reciting the Patimokkha, reciting the Three Refuges, and ordination ceremonies. Each Buddhist sect, too, has an association with a particular teaching that is chanted during ceremonies.

As in ancient times, chanting for Buddhists today is a way of showing their commitment to the Dhamma, and of sharing their commitment with others. It is an inclusive practice: anyone can do it, as it requires no special skills. It has a very calming effect on the mind, because of the regular rhythm, and so can be used in preparation for meditation. Finally, it is a way for Buddhists to feel connected not only with those members of the Sangha who are with them, but with all those followers of the Dhamma from former ages who chanted the same teachings.

Some Buddhist sects chant short phrases over and over again. These are sometimes called **mantras**. Although they have a literal, word-for-word meaning, their true meaning is much

deeper. Some believe that reciting the phrase in itself is sufficient to reveal enlightenment. In this case, the phrase is a sort of kasina, a meditation object.

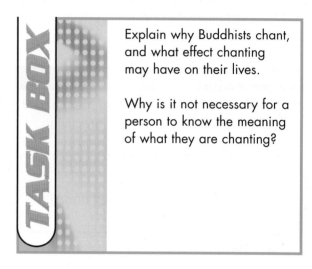

TASK BOX

Explain why Buddhists chant, and what effect chanting may have on their lives.

Why is it not necessary for a person to know the meaning of what they are chanting?

We have seen, for example, that members of the Pure Land sect chant the phrase Namu Amida Butsu. The phrase is called Nembutsu. Literally it means, 'I dedicate my life to the Buddha of Infinite Light', though each word of this sentence has further and deeper meanings. Many Pure Land Buddhists would say, however, that the meaning of the Nembutsu is less important than chanting it. The act of chanting it can bring you to the Pure Land even if you do not know what it means.

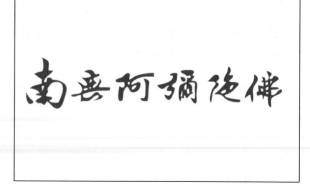

▲ Namu Amida Butsu in Japanese.

In the same way, the Nichiren sects of Japan chant Nam (or Namu) Myoho Renge Kyo. Roughly, this means, 'I dedicate my life to the Dharma and the law of cause and effect (karma) in eternity'. This phrase is called the Daimoku. Daimoku can be chanted as a meditation object in itself, or it can be chanted to an object. For some Nichiren Buddhists, the object of concentration is called the Gohonzon, and is a paper scroll or wooden panel inscribed with Chinese and Sanskrit characters representing every aspect of life, including buddhahood.

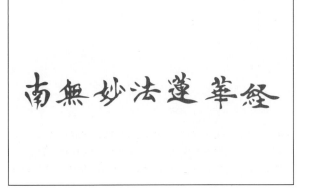

▲ Nam(u) Myoho Renge Kyo in classical Chinese.

One of the most famous mantras is Om Mani Padme Hum from the Tibetan tradition. Tibetan Buddhists believe that chanting, saying, whispering, reading or even just seeing the phrase will bring great blessings from the Buddha of Compassion. For Tibetan Buddhists, Om Mani Padme Hum includes all of the teachings of Buddhism. Like other mantras, it does have a literal meaning, which is sometimes expressed as, 'Hail to the jewel of the lotus'.

▲ Om Mani Padme Hum in Tibetan script.

The syllable OM is a very ancient religious symbol. It stands for reality itself, for the goal of the spiritual path. It also includes the idea of opening up to freedom, and is said to describe the idea that the infinite can be found within each individual.

MANI means 'jewel', and represents the enlightened mind. Just as possessing a precious jewel can remove poverty, so the enlightened mind removes the difficulties of living in Samsara.

PADME represents the lotus. This powerful symbol of Buddhism grows in muddy waters. The muddier the water, the stronger and more beautiful the flower. It shows that enlightenment springs in ordinary human beings in the world of Samsara.

HUM (pronounced 'hoong') represents that which is immoveable, invariable, stable and dependable.

Silence is used by some Buddhists, especially Zen Buddhists, to train the mind. A Zen retreat generally lasts for a week, and is conducted in silence. There are three purposes to it. First, it is a way of calming and clearing the mind. You do not have to think about responses in conversations, or about what other people mean by what they say. Second, it is a way of getting to know yourself better, recognising both strengths and faults. Third, it is a way of training you to communicate with others without relying on words, and to feel a oneness with them.

TEST YOURSELF

1 What is a mantra?
2 Why is it necessary to understand the meaning of a mantra when chanting it?

HOW DO LAY BUDDHISTS WORSHIP?

Many lay Buddhists practise puja at home, and some rarely, if ever, visit temples to worship. They have shrines at home where they worship. The layout of the shrine and the objects associated with it vary from one branch of Buddhism to another, but there are some common features, each with a symbolic meaning.

▼ Three Buddhist shrines. Notice the common features, such as the statue of the Buddha, the flowers, candles and incense.

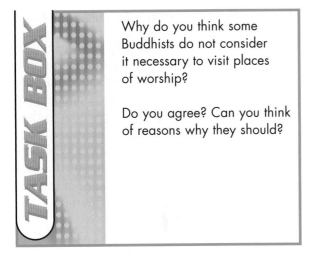

Why do you think some Buddhists do not consider it necessary to visit places of worship?

Do you agree? Can you think of reasons why they should?

Common features of a Buddhist shrine

■ There is usually at least one statue or picture of the Buddha in the centre of the shrine. Some have a whole variety of Buddha images. Buddhists do not worship the statues, but use them to reflect on the qualities of the buddha nature to reveal them in themselves.

■ Vegetation takes the form of flowers or evergreen leaves. The life of a flower is very short, and within a matter of days it will open up, bloom, fade, then shrivel and die. It will, however, leave seeds for regeneration. It symbolises anicca and life in Samsara. Some Buddhist sects prefer to use evergreen leaves on their shrines as a symbol of eternity.

■ A small pot of water is usually placed on the shrine. Water is essential for life, and so is a precious commodity. It must be pure. It is, therefore, a symbol of a pure respect and reverence for life.

■ A candle that lights up the shrine is a conspicuous symbol of enlightenment.

■ Buddhists burn incense on their shrines as it purifies the air. As the sweet-smelling smoke spreads through the atmosphere, it symbolises the Dhamma, the law of life, operating in the universe.

■ Fruit is offered at most shrines, representing the interdependent nature of all things. Our lives depend on what the earth produces, and the welfare of the world depends on us. Offering natural produce is a way of expressing gratitude.

■ Most Buddhists use a bell to indicate the beginning or end of the various parts of the puja. It can be seen as a symbol of kamma, the law of cause and effect: the harder you hit the bell, the louder it rings. The bell is often placed on a cushion shaped like a lotus flower. The lotus is, itself, a symbol of kamma since it produces seeds and flowers at the same time. This indicates the Buddhist belief that the effect of what you do is determined at the same time as you do it.

■ A shrine is likely to have photographs of great Buddhist teachers, or paintings of teachers from the distant past, or relatives, alive or deceased. They enable the Buddhist to focus on spreading positive feelings of love, peace and well-being to those people.

■ Books of teachings that are recited or chanted will be on or near the shrine.

Draw and label a diagram of a Buddhist shrine.

Use the images on page 86, and collect images from other sources to help you. Underneath your diagram, explain how a shrine helps a Buddhist to worship.

Some Buddhist shrines, especially in the Tibetan tradition, just have seven water bowls to represent all the offerings on a shrine. This comes from the Indian custom, still practised today, of offering eight hospitalities to a guest at one's home: water for drinking, water for washing one's feet, flowers, incense, illumination, scented lotion, fruit and music.

Puja may be described as a celebration of life, and so the objects that are found on a Buddhist shrine can represent the things that are essential for sustaining life: water, food, shelter, light and warmth. They can therefore be seen as objects to stimulate the five senses:

- Taste is stimulated by water and food.
- Sight is stimulated by candlelight.
- Smell is stimulated by the fragrance of incense.
- Hearing is stimulated by the sound of the bell.
- Touch is stimulated by the use of prayer beads (which are described later in this Unit).

The way we treat things is an indication of how we feel about them. A shrine is always treated with great care out of respect. A Buddhist would say that his or her shrine reflects the state of his or her mind, and could even influence it. So he or she would want to ensure that the shrine is kept clean and tidy to help the mind to be clear and uncluttered. The shrine is cleaned every day; the water, fruit and vegetation are changed daily. The time that it takes to do this is seen as an opportunity to focus the mind on one's spiritual progress.

WHY DO BUDDHISTS BOW BEFORE A SHRINE?

Bowing is a very important symbolic gesture in most Buddhist countries. In Japan, for example, children bow to their teachers and even their parents; lay people bow to priests and monks; the young bow to the old; workers bow to their bosses. Lowering your head to put yourself in a lower position than someone else is a symbol of humility. It is an acknowledgement that the other person has a greater experience of life, or a deeper understanding of spiritual matters.

Your head contains all your ideas, your beliefs, your feelings. It also has a face that makes you instantly identifiable. For Buddhists, then, bowing one's head also indicates the denial of the ego (anatta).

TASK BOX

Explain how Buddhists use their bodies in worship.

First of all, look through the photographs in this book, and make a note of those that show pictures of people: kneeling, sitting in the lotus position, prostrating, standing, walking, circumambulating. Then explain the meaning and purpose of each.

▲ A Buddhist prostrating himself.

When Buddhists bow before a shrine, they usually do so three times, in recognition of the Three Treasures – the Buddha, the Dhamma and the Sangha. It is usually done from a kneeling position. Hands are held together at the head, lips and chest, symbolising respect in thought, word and deed. Sometimes worshippers push themselves forward until they are lying full-length on the ground before a shrine. It is a sign of devotion, commitment and personal dedication. The practice is called prostration.

When Buddhists bow before images of the Buddha, they are not worshipping him. The statue is just a symbol of the highest human qualities. In bowing to the statue, Buddhists are acknowledging the value of these qualities, recognising that they have the potential to reveal them, and creating the circumstances for that to happen. It keeps them mindful of the reasons why they go to the shrine.

▲ Mala.

These must be overcome if one is to reveal one's buddhahood. They therefore symbolise the ordinary world of Samsara, and the belief that human beings become enlightened in this world. On some mala the 108 beads are separated into three sections by three larger beads. These represent the Three Treasures – the Buddha, the Dhamma and the Sangha. On others, the Three Treasures are represented by tassels.

Mala are usually held between the palms of the hands while a Buddhist is chanting. They may be used to count the number of times a mantra has been chanted. Some Buddhists believe that they have a symbolic power to drive away worldly desires. For most, the physical feeling of having the beads pressed into their hands is a reminder of the purpose of puja. In other words, it is an aid to mindfulness.

Originally, mala were made from the seeds of the bodhi pipal (fig) tree. Today they may be made of almost any material, though polished wood is most common. It is said that Josei Toda, once the leader of the Soka Gakkai in Japan, made a set of beads out of milk-bottle tops when he was in prison for opposing the Japanese participation in the Second World War. Prayer beads are called juzu in Japan. Some Tibetan prayer beads are made of semi-precious stones, or even the bones of a deceased lama. On Tibetan beads the pieces at the end of the tassels represent a **vajra** (dorje) and a bell (ghanta).

TEST YOURSELF

1 What objects are commonly found on a Buddhist shrine?
2 What do the seven water pots on a Tibetan shrine represent?
3 How and why do Buddhists look after their shrines?
4 What is the purpose of bowing before a shrine?

WHAT DO BUDDHISTS USE TO HELP THEM WORSHIP?

Mala

When Buddhists worship, particularly if they are chanting, they use prayer beads to help them to concentrate and keep them mindful. Beads are used by worshippers in a number of religious traditions. In Buddhism they are called **mala**. The mala used in different sects vary in both design and construction, but there are common features.

Most mala consist of 108 beads strung in a loop. The beads represent the 108 worldly desires.

Vajra

The vajra is an important symbol in Tantric Buddhism. The word 'vajra' means two things:

■ Diamond – a hard jewel, which can cut anything else, but cannot itself be cut.
■ Thunderbolt – a symbol of power.

It is like a weapon that will always destroy the enemy, always return to the hand of the person who uses it, and cannot be stopped from achieving what is needed. The vajra therefore represents the determination to cut through illusion and to achieve enlightenment.

The vajra itself is a handle, usually made of brass. In the centre of it is a sphere. Its perfect and complete shape represents the whole of reality. Out of that sphere come two lotus flowers, one growing upwards, the other downwards. The lotus represents growth, and the two of them show that there are two ways of interpreting and responding to reality, one positive and the other negative.

From each of these flowers come five spokes – one in the centre and four at each of the compass points. The spokes at the top symbolise the Five Buddhas: five types of wisdom that a person should develop before becoming enlightened. The ones at the bottom represent the Five Elements (earth, water, fire, air, spirit), the Five Khandhas (see p. 15), and also the Five Poisons (infatuation, hatred, conceit, passion and envy).

There are poisons at one end and wisdoms at the other – so the vajra is a symbol of the determination to transform all of life into something positive. The poisons are not ignored, nor does a person pretend that they do not exist; but their energy is converted into something more creative and positive. Some medicines are made from poisonous substances; yet, in the hands of a skilled doctor, they can be used to cure. Buddhists believe that, in the same way, a person's negative tendencies can be used to produce spiritual benefits.

Prayer wheels

Tibetan Buddhists have other devices to enable them to receive spiritual benefits and to spread those benefits to others. One such object is the prayer wheel. Prayer wheels (known as mani wheels) are cylinders that contain pieces of paper on which are written the mantra Om Mani Padme Hum many, many times. The paper is wrapped around a central axle that can be turned by rotating the cylindrical container.

We have seen that Tibetan Buddhists believe that they receive blessings each time they chant Om Mani Padme Hum. They also believe that they can receive the same blessings each time a prayer wheel is turned; and, since the wheel can be turned faster than you can chant, blessings are multiplied.

Prayer wheels can be small and portable, and people spin them while walking. Others are large and fixed, and people turn them with their hands as they pass them. They are always spun clockwise (if seen from above), so that the words of the mantra move in the right order.

▲ A vajra.

A New Approach – Buddhism

▲ Small prayer wheels are carried in the hand and rotated.

▲ Large prayer wheels are fixed and people rotate them as they pass.

▲ Tibetan prayer flags.

Some prayer wheels work automatically, for example by being turned by running water, or by the wind. Some even say that having the words Om Mani Padme Hum on the hard drive of your computer will produce benefits as it spins!

Prayer flags

The power of the wind to spread blessings is also used in prayer flags. These are banners on which are written mantras and texts. They are strung together and hung from trees or any structure so that the wind can blow the blessings of the Buddha of Compassion throughout the world.

TASK BOX

Explain how and why Buddhists use artefacts in worship.

You should describe the use of bells, vajra, mala, mani wheels and prayer flags, and give reasons for their use.

A New Approach – Buddhism

WHY ARE THERE SO MANY DIFFERENT IMAGES OF THE BUDDHA?

A statue or image of the Buddha used as an object of contemplation or worship is called a **rupa**. It is important to understand from the outset that a rupa is not meant to represent the historical Buddha, but rather the qualities of enlightenment in a human being. So the reason why there is such a great variety of Buddha rupas is that each represents a different characteristic of buddhahood: wisdom, compassion, courage, determination, patience, generosity, and so on.

Buddha rupas also vary in form and style from country to country and from culture to culture. The physical characteristics of the Buddha portrayed on a statue are likely to reflect those of the people who made it. Over the centuries, each country has developed its own style of rupa, but the imagery of them remains consistent.

Traditionally there are 32 characteristics of the Buddha represented on a rupa. Some of them are:

- Religious symbols – for example, the curl or dot on his forehead, which represents the sixth cakra (energy centre). It is called the urna.
- Ancient Indian fashion – for example, the top-knot in his hair.
- Representations of the historical Buddha – for example, Siddattha is reputed to have had curly hair.
- Social symbols – for example, his long ear-lobes signify Siddattha's princely status. Wealthy people in ancient times, as today, showed their wealth by wearing gold jewellery. Royalty wore heavy gold earrings that stretched the lobes.
- Symbols whose origins are unknown – for example, three rings around his neck.

As Buddhists chant, meditate and make offerings to Buddha rupas, they reflect on the qualities of enlightenment. Their religious practices before the rupas are intended to reveal those same qualities in themselves.

▲ Buddha rupas are loaded with symbolism.

What do the hand gestures on Buddha rupas mean?

Human beings use their hands to communicate in all sorts of ways. Without speaking, people can use their hands to say, 'Hello,' or, 'Well done!' or, 'Come here,' or, 'Go away!'. Entire language systems have been developed for people to communicate using only the hands. The use of hand gestures is a very powerful means of communication. You can 'feel' what a gesture means, rather than just understand it.

Buddhists use gestures in two ways. They are used on Buddha rupas to help express what the particular image stands for; and they are used in puja to keep the worshipper mindful of the focus of his or her reflection. They are called **mudras**.

There are seven commonly used mudras. Most of them stem from events in the Buddha's life, but each has a unique meaning.

Earth-touching (Bumispara)

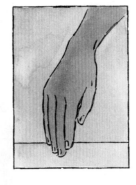

Buddhists believe that the Buddha, just before he became enlightened, called on the earth to bear witness to his right to be enlightened. He reached down and touched the ground with his fingertips.

It is a gesture that accepts everything as it is – it 'touches the earth', starts from the reality of things here and now. It is associated with a particular kind of wisdom – the wisdom of a mirror. It is the wisdom to see yourself clearly, as you really are. It may be used at the beginning of meditation to 'root' the meditator, to start from the person's present situation in the world.

Generosity (Varada)

It is said that the Buddha met a social outcast called Sunita. Sunita immediately recognised his compassion, and lay before him in humility. The Buddha showed his generosity, and extended his hand downwards, palm outwards.

This mudra represents the wisdom of equality – treating everybody with equal respect for their dignity. Giving (dana) is an important quality for a Buddhist to cultivate.

Meditation (Dhyana)

Siddattha Gotama was an expert at meditation. He learned from the masters of his day, and became a great teacher himself. He was practising seated meditation when he became enlightened.

If you sit cross legged on the floor, the most natural position for the hands to fall is in your lap, palms uppermost, one on top of the other. It is perfectly balanced and relaxed. The hands show that you are receptive and open to all the eternal qualities. Meditation allows the Dhamma to become the natural way to think, feel and act for Buddhists.

Fearlessness (Abhaya)

The Buddha had a cousin, Devadatta, who was jealous of him. He attempted to kill him three times. On one of these occasions, he got an elephant drunk and made it stampede in Siddattha's direction. The Buddha raised his hand, palm outwards, towards the elephant, who stopped and submitted to him.

This mudra shows determination and courage. It is the wisdom to overcome obstacles by using loving kindness (metta) and compassion (karuna).

Turning the Wheel of the Law (Dhamma-cakka)

When the Buddha gave his first sermon in the Deer Park at Sarnath, it is said that he taught about the Four Noble Truths. It is called Turning the Wheel of the Law.

Two circles are made by connecting the forefinger with the thumb of each hand. The other fingers are outstretched. The circle represents the Wheel of the Law, while the four fingers of each hand represent the Four Noble Truths. The eight fingers of both hands represent the Noble Eightfold Path. The mudra is formed in front of the chest, close to the heart, where people experience deep emotions.

Teaching (Vitarka)

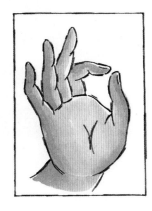

This is half of the Dhamma-cakka Mudra. It is formed using the right hand. The thumb is usually touching the forefinger – the first Noble Truth – but sometimes it connects with the second, third or fourth finger, which represent the other Noble Truths.

Respect (Anjali)

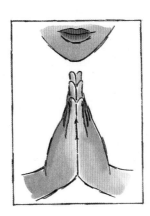

This is a common gesture of greeting in the East. It welcomes an equal. For this reason, it is rarely seen on a Buddha rupa, since unenlightened human beings are not seen by Buddhists as equal to the Buddha. It symbolises respect for all beings.

TEST YOURSELF

1. What are mala used for?
2. What does the vajra symbolise in Tibetan Buddhism?
3. What is a Buddha rupa?
4. What do the following mudras represent? Abhaya, Anjali, Bumispara, Dhyana, Varada, Vitarka.

WHAT ARE BODHISATTVAS?

As the Mahayana movement grew and contributed to the development of the Vajrayana, so did the mythology of Buddhism. Great Bodhisattvas (enlightenment beings) came to be seen as supernatural figures symbolising spiritual qualities. They became focuses of worship as beings who could save people – even whole countries.

Images of the Bodhisattvas and Buddhas in the Mahayana and Vajrayana traditions function as more than reminders of their spiritual qualities. These Buddhists see the images as actually possessing the spirit and power of the beings they represent. They therefore hold a position of honour in worship. Sometimes scriptures or relics are placed inside them; sometimes they are given internal organs modelled out of clay.

Avalokitesvara

The most popular of the Great Bodhisattvas is Avalokitesvara. He is a symbol of compassion: in fact his Sanskrit name means 'The Lord Who Looks Down (with compassion)'. His image stretches right across the Mahayana countries. In China, 'he' is female and is called Kwan-shih-yin, which means 'The One Who Takes Notice of the Cries of the World'. The Japanese name, Kannon, comes from this. So widely known and respected is Kannon that the Canon electrical and photographic company is named after him/her. Buddhists throughout the East worship and pray to Avalokitesvara in their daily lives. In Tibet, Avalokitesvara is male, and is known as Chenrezig.

There are many stories about Avalokitesvara in the Buddhist scriptures. In one, he is one of the Buddha's attendants. In another, he is said to take on 39 different forms to save the people. In Chinese art he sometimes appears as a bull, warning a butcher away from his murderous livelihood.

Pictures and rupas of Avalokitesvara show him crowned like a prince and dressed in royal garments. He holds a lotus bud in his hand to show that all human beings can 'bloom' as buddhas. Sometimes his hands are cupped together, like a lotus bud, to indicate his willingness to grant wishes to all those who call upon him. Other images show him with 1000 arms: this means that he is there in every situation, each hand ready to help.

▲ Avalokitesvara.

Manjusri

Manjusri means 'Sweet Glory'. If Avalokitesvara represents the Buddha's compassion, then Manjusri represents his wisdom. His special task is to destroy ignorance and delusion, and awaken spiritual knowledge and wisdom (prajna).

He is therefore depicted as holding a lotus supporting a copy of the Prajna Paramita Sutras (Teachings on the Perfection of Wisdom). In his other hand he is wielding a flaming sword: wisdom cutting away ignorance. His function is to protect teachers of the Dharma.

▲ Manjusri.

Manjusri is therefore a spiritual guide. He is said to have been the teacher of all the buddhas of the past, including Siddattha Gotama, and will be the guide of Maitreya, the Buddha-to-be. He is also described as the father and mother of all the bodhisattvas.

Maitreya

In some Buddhist traditions, the time in which the Dhamma is followed is divided into three periods. In the first, the Dhamma is taught and accepted. In the second, the Dhamma is practiced. In the third period (mappo, in Japanese), Buddhist teachings will cease to have any effect. A new Buddha will appear who will teach the Dhamma appropriate for the age of mappo. The Buddha-to-be is a bodhisattva at present, and is called Maitreya.

Maitreya means 'the Kindly One', and is the only one of the Great Bodhisattvas to be recognised by the Theravada school.

In China, Maitreya is known as Mi-lo-fo, and is often shown as a large, jolly, pot-bellied man carrying a sack of presents for children. The sack is called pu-tai, and Mi-lo-fo is sometimes named after this sack. In the West he is better known as 'The Laughing Buddha'.

▲ Maitreya, known as Mi-lo-fo in China and 'The Laughing Buddha' in the West.

Amitabha

We have already come across Amitabha when we looked at Pure Land Buddhism in Unit Two. The Japanese priest, Shinran, believed that Amitabha Buddha's purpose in making his 48 vows to save all people was particularly to save the wicked. The more wretched the human being, the greater is Amitabha's determination to save him or her.

Pure Land Buddhists reflect on their faults to become aware of their ignorance. Then they are able to pray to Amitabha to free them from their suffering. Amitabha has vowed to save everyone and anyone who calls upon him.

As Amida, he is very popular in Japan. Some statues of him are among the largest statues in world.

▲ Amitabha.

Tara

Tara is another Tibetan expression of compassion, this time definitely female. She is sometimes shown as green in colour; sometimes she is white.

▲ Tara.

Vajrapani

Vajrapani, 'The Wrathful One', expresses energy in pursuit of the good. He is a Tibetan deity who tramples underfoot all obstacles to enlightenment. He shows great determination, and a recognition that controlled anger can be used as a force for good.

▲ Vajrapani.

TASK BOX

Explain why Buddhists use so many different images in their worship. Give examples to illustrate your answer.

TEST YOURSELF

A B C

1 Why are images of Bodhisattvas and Buddhas important in Mahayana worship?
2 What does Avalokitesvara represent?
3 Who does the 'Laughing Buddha' represent?
4 Which Bodhisattva represents anger?

A New Approach – Buddhism

🕸 http://www.buddhanet.net/metta_au.htm *Audio instructions on metta samatha.*
🕸 http://www.do-not-zzz.com/ *A spectacular site, explaining the principles and practice of meditation in Zen Buddhism.*
🕸 http://www.rebirthingonline.com/htms/lama.html *A simple Tibetan meditation exercise.*
🕸 http://www.artnetwork.com/Mandala/gallery.html *The process of making a sand mandala.*
🕸 http://www.everlife.org/gateway.htm#sound *Provides an audio file of Nam Myoho Renge Kyo.*
🕸 http://nichirenscoffeehouse.net/GohonzonShu/001.html *Photographs of Gohonzons.*
🕸 http://www.ommanipadmehum.com/ *Audio file of Om Mani Padme Hum.*
🕸 http://www.dharma-haven.org/tibetan/meaning-of-om-mani-padme-hung.htm *Detailed explanation of Om Mani Padme Hum.*
🕸 http://www.dharmaforkids.com/Buddha/symbol/buddhasymbol.htm *Find out about the symbols of a Buddha rupa interactively.*

WEBLINKS

REMEMBER

▶ The word rupa means 'form'.
▶ Although Buddhists worship in front of Buddha rupas, they do not worship the Buddha.
▶ Many Buddhists worship at home before a shrine.
▶ Buddhists use their bodies symbolically during worship.
▶ Chanting is part of most Buddhist puja.
▶ Different sects chant different Suttas/Sutras and mantras.
▶ For some Mahayana Buddhists, chanting a mantra replaces the Noble Eightfold Path.
▶ The word bodhisattva means 'enlightenment being'.
▶ Bodhisattvas represent the highest qualities human beings can develop.

---

1 a) Write a detailed description of how Buddhists worship. (8 marks)

b) Explain why Buddhists make offerings at shrines. (7 marks)

c) 'You cannot influence events by praying about them. You have to take action.'
Do you agree? Give reasons for your answer, showing that you have thought about more than one point of view. (5 marks)

2 a) Describe the main features of a Buddha rupa. (8 marks)

b) Explain why Buddhists meditate. (7 marks)

c) 'Right Concentration is the most important step on the Noble Eightfold Path.'
Do you agree? Give reasons to support your answer and show that you have thought about different points of view. (5 marks)

Assignment

KEY WORDS

Abhidhamma (Pali), Abhidharma (Sanskrit): A section of the Tipitaka that gives philosophical and psychological explanations of the Dhamma.

Canon: The accepted Buddhist scriptures.

Dhammapada: A Buddhist scripture containing 423 sayings attributed to the Buddha.

Jataka: 'Lives', stories of the Buddha's previous lives.

Prajna: 'Wisdom'.

Sunyata: 'Emptiness', the nature of things that have no fixed identity.

Sutta (Pali), Sutra (Sanskrit): 'Thread', a text giving a teaching.

Tantra: 'Pattern', mystic writings in Tibetan Buddhism.

Tipitaka (Pali), Tripitaka (Sanskrit): 'Three Baskets', the three collections of Buddhist texts: the Vinaya, the Suttas and the Abhidhamma.

Vinaya: The rules of discipline for monks and nuns.

WHICH WRITINGS ARE SPECIAL FOR BUDDHISTS?

KEY QUESTION

How are the Buddha's teachings passed on?

During his lifetime, the Buddha travelled around teaching about the Dhamma. As he did so, an ever-increasing number of people joined him as disciples. These were the first bhikkhus: the monastic Sangha. As the Sangha grew and viharas were set up, it became necessary to establish rules of behaviour, especially after women were allowed to join. The Buddha's teachings and the rules of the monastic Sangha, together with explanations of the Buddha's teachings, form the writings that are still special for Theravadin Buddhists today. These three sets of scriptures are written in the Pali language, and, in English, are known as the Pali **Canon**. Buddhists call them the **Tipitaka**.

As Buddhism spread towards the Far East, and Mahayana Buddhism developed, new ideas became part of the religion. These new ideas were written down as teachings of the Buddha.

Mahayana Buddhists accept the authority of the Tipitaka (which they call Tripitaka in Sanskrit). In addition they developed thousands of their own texts. Some have a special significance to the various Mahayana sects. They include the Diamond Sutra, the Lotus Sutra, the Heart Sutra and the Pure Land Sutra.

Tibetan Buddhists also accept the Theravada scriptures and the Mahayana writings. In addition, there are writings that have unique importance for Tibetan Buddhists. These include Tantric texts and commentaries on them; stories, poetry and plays; works on logic, language, medicine, science, astrology and art.

TEST YOURSELF

1 What does 'Tipitaka' mean?
2 What sorts of writings are contained in the Tipitaka?
3 What else is the Tipitaka known as?
4 Which Sutras are especially important to Mahayana Buddhists?

How were the Buddhist scriptures collected?

Like any good teacher, the Buddha suited his teachings to the capabilities of his pupils. He would teach in one way to dedicated bhikkhus and in another way to simple lay believers, so that everyone would be able to grasp his meaning at one level or another.

At a time when few people were educated, and when religious teachings were not put into writing, it was common for people to retain a lot of information in their heads. Perhaps this is why so many Buddhist teachings are in the form of lists (the Three Universal Truths, the Four Noble Truths, the Five Precepts, and so on). People committed the Buddha's teachings to memory and passed them on to others exactly as they heard them. The teachings are called **Suttas**.

As the bhikkhus grew in numbers, it became their responsibility to remember the Suttas and pass them on to others exactly as they heard them. This is why many of them start with the words, 'Thus I heard'.

For 20 years, the bhikkhus lived together without any rules, but as time went on, situations occurred that made it necessary to introduce them. As each new situation arose, the Buddha called the bhikkhus together to decide on a new rule. Once this was done, they would recite all the rules together to memorise them. They are called the **Vinaya**.

With the passage of time, the circumstances of the Buddha's teachings were forgotten, and some of the sermons became more difficult to understand fully. Later Buddhists had to interpret and explain the teachings. These commentaries were also committed to memory, and are known as the **Abhidhamma**.

The Vinaya and the Suttas were first agreed upon three months after the Buddha's death when the surviving bhikkhus met at the First Council. The Abhidhamma, meanwhile, continued its development.

TASK BOX

Describe how the Buddha's teaching came to be written down.

You will need to use information from this Unit and Unit Two.

The Vinaya, the Suttas and the Abhidhamma were finally written down after the meeting of the Fourth Council. Each was called a pitaka, meaning 'basket'. It refers to the practice of using baskets to pass materials from one person to another on a building site. The Vinaya Pitaka, the Sutta Pitaka and the Abhidhamma Pitaka together form the Tipitaka: the Three Baskets.

▲ The three baskets.

TEST YOURSELF

1. What are the three pitakas called?
2. What does 'pitaka' mean?
3. Why do many Suttas start with the words, 'Thus I heard'?
4. What is the Abhidhamma?

WHY IS THE VINAYA PITAKA IMPORTANT TO BUDDHISTS?

The word 'Vinaya' literally means 'discipline by leading away from faults'. The Vinaya Pitaka, therefore, contains the rules of behaviour that bhikkhus and bhikkhunis are expected to keep. They describe offences that may be committed and the punishment that will be applied for each offence. Their purpose is to lead bhikkhus away from the kind of behaviour that disrupts life in a monastery. More generally, they enable bhikkhus to become aware of how their thoughts, words and actions affect those around them.

When the first bhikkhus were ordained, and for some time afterwards, rules were not thought to be necessary. However, on one occasion, it was discovered that a bhikkhu had slept with his ex-wife. Of course, this was not illegal, and perhaps not immoral, but it was clear that the bhikkhu in question was not mindful of the path to Nibbana. The Buddha believed that the time was right to introduce some regulations.

Later, when the first women were ordained as bhikkhunis, the Buddha realised that tensions might form between them and the bhikkhus. The women had to follow the same rules as the men, but others were laid down specifically for them. Altogether, there are 227 rules for bhikkhus and 311 for bhikkhunis. These are the Patimokkha rules that bhikkhus recite each Uposatha Day.

Each of the Patimokkha rules was made as a result of an incident that occurred. The Vinaya Pitaka describes each incident as an introduction to the rule. This emphasises that the rules are all grounded in the realities of life. The rules are classified according to the appropriate punishment.

The four most serious offences deserve being expelled from the Sangha, never to return:

- Sexual intercourse.
- Stealing.
- Intentionally killing another human being.
- Making untrue claims about spiritual achievements.

There are 13 offences that deserve temporary suspension from the Sangha. They include:

- Three offences of sexual contact.
- Matchmaking.
- Causing conflict between others.

There are two offences, the punishment for which has to be decided on a case-by-case basis:

- Sitting alone with a woman in private.
- Sitting alone with a woman in public.

Thirty offences are caused by greed for possessions. The punishment is to give up the possession and promise to the other bhikkhus not to repeat the offence. Examples include:

- Accepting money.
- Having too many robes.

The remaining offences require the bhikkhu concerned to confess his fault to another bhikkhu. Examples are:

- Lying.
- Intentionally damaging a living plant.
- Making fun of another bhikkhu.

There are also instructions about how to handle disputes, for example if a bhikkhu denies that he has committed the offence of which he is accused.

TASK BOX

'The Vinaya comes from another age: it has no relevance for bhikkhus today.'

Do you agree? Give reasons to support your answer and show that you have thought about different points of view.

The Vinaya Pitaka is made up of five books:

1. Parajika Pali
2. Pacittiya Pali
} The first two books contain the Patimokkha rules.

3. Mahavaggi Pali
4. Culavagga Pali
} The third and fourth books contain information about ordination, how to conduct ceremonies and how to carry out punishments.

5. Paravira Pali
} The fifth book is a manual providing information about how to observe the Vinaya.

WHY IS THE SUTTA PITAKA IMPORTANT FOR BUDDHISTS?

The word 'Sutta' means 'thread'. The Sutta Pitaka refers to the collection of the Buddha's teachings. Just as a thread is used to mark out a flowerbed and protect the flowers from harm, so the Suttas set out the Dhamma as the Buddha taught it, and protect the teachings from corruption.

Altogether there are nearly 20,000 Suttas. They were compiled at the Fourth Council of the Sangha, which was held in 84 BCE in Sri Lanka. After the wording of the Suttas was agreed upon, they were written onto palm leaves. The task took 12 years. It is said that, if the leaves were placed on top of each other, they would exceed the height of 15 elephants. Today they are published in 45 volumes.

Most of the Suttas are written as dialogues: discussions between the Buddha and his bhikkhus, or sometimes with lay people. In this way the same teachings are presented in different ways, according to the audience's ability to understand. They start with the words, 'Thus I heard,' and then describe the circumstances in which the teaching took place. The end usually states how delighted the Buddha's audience was with the teaching.

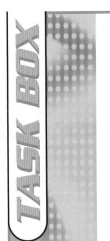

TASK BOX

Explain why the Suttas are important to householder (lay) Buddhists today.

You should consider the range of subjects the Suttas cover and the uses to which they are put.

▲ This is an ancient Buddhist text. Tibetan Buddhist scriptures are still made to look like palm leaves.

Since the Suttas set out the Buddha's teachings in a variety of different ways and on a variety of levels, they are still used as teaching aids today. Buddhists use them for studying particular aspects of the Dhamma, and they are used to illustrate lectures and writings on the range of Buddhist principles. Many form the basis of study in themselves.

But the Suttas are not just objects of learning. For Buddhists, they are a foundation of faith.

Passages from them are recited or chanted in ceremonies with the aim of developing a deeper understanding of the Dhamma and how it can be used in daily life.

The Suttas cover a variety of subjects:

- Some explain the theoretical principles of the Dhamma.
- Some give practical guidance on how to practise the Dhamma in everyday life.
- Some outline the ways in which lay Buddhists should support the monastic Sangha.
- Some set out expectations of moral behaviour (sila).
- Some give practical instructions on meditation techniques.

The Suttas are divided into five sections, or Nikayas:

- The Digha Nikaya (Long Teachings) contains 34 Suttas, including teachings on mindfulness (Mahasatipatthana Sutta); on morality, concentration and wisdom (Subha Sutta); on dependent origination (Mahanidrana Sutta); on the roots and causes of wrong views (Brahmajala Sutta); and a long description of the Buddha's last days (Mahaparinibbana Sutta).

- The Majjhima Nikaya (Medium-Length Teachings) contains 152 Suttas that cover the complete range of the Buddha's teachings. He uses reasoned argument, and parables and similes to make the Dhamma relevant to his audience.
- The Samyutta Nikaya (Themed Teachings) contains 7762 Suttas put into 56 groups within five 'vaggas' or sections. Each vagga deals with a separate theme. The first describes the circumstances of the teachings; the second deals with dependent origination (the chain of cause and effect that links all things); the third explains the Universal Truth of anatta; the fourth explains the Universal Truth of anicca; the fifth describes, in more general terms, Buddhist philosophy.
- The Anguttara Nikaya (Adding-one-each-time Teachings) contains 9557 short Suttas in 11 groups. The peculiar title of the Nikaya comes from the subject matter of each of the groups. The first contains teachings about single items of the Dhamma (the 'Ones'); the second contains teachings about double items of the Dhamma (the 'Twos'); and so one, up to 11. The Nikaya provides a complete summary of Buddhist teachings on psychology and human behaviour.

PERSPECTIVES

It is unlikely that all of the Suttas contain the words of the Buddha, Siddattha Gotama. One Buddhist explained it in this way:

'You needn't worry about whether or not the words in the Suttas were actually uttered by the historical Buddha (no one can ever prove this either way). Just keep in mind that the teachings in the Suttas have been practised – with apparent success – by countless followers for some 2600 years. If you want to know whether or not the teachings really work, then study the Suttas and put their teachings into practice and find out, first-hand, for yourself.'

What do you think? Does it matter if the Suttas are not direct teachings of the Buddha?

You will need to refer to Buddhist beliefs about the nature of buddhahood to answer this question.

- The Khuddaka Nikaya (Minor Teachings) contains 15 Suttas, which, in spite of the title of the section, are some of the most widely read. The Nikaya includes two of the most famous books in the whole Tipitaka: the **Dhammapada** and the **Jataka**.

TEST YOURSELF

1 What does Vinaya mean?
2 Why are there more rules for nuns than monks?
3 What are Suttas?
4 How are the Suttas used in Buddhist worship?

Dhammapada

Dhammapada means 'Pieces of the Dhamma'. It comprises 423 verses divided into 26 chapters. Each chapter contains a number of verses, which consist of short sayings, each verse describing an aspect of Buddhist teaching, or a general observation about the nature of life. They are thought to have been spoken by the Buddha at various times during his teaching career. Unlike the other teachings of the Sutta Pitaka, the teachings of the Dhammapada have no context: there is no description of the circumstances in which they were spoken.

Not all of the sayings are obviously religious. Some offer general guidance on how human beings can live in peace with each other:

> Everyone is afraid of violence; everyone fears death. If you put yourself in someone else's place, you should not kill or cause another person to kill. (129)
>
> Hatred does not stop hatred: only love stops it. This is an ancient law. (5)
>
> Don't look for faults in others, in what they have done or not done; look at what you have done and not done. (50)

Some of the sayings take this further and explain that actions made now will have consequences in the future (kamma):

> If anyone hurts an innocent person, the evil of that will come back to that fool just like dust thrown into the wind. (125)
>
> Do not ignore evil thinking, 'It will not come to me'. A water pot is filled drop by drop; in the same way, the fool fills himself with evil little by little. (121)
>
> There is nowhere on earth – not in the sky, nor in the sea, nor in a mountain cave – that one may escape from the effects of one's evil deeds. (127)

TASK BOX

Evaluate the first six verses from the Dhammapada on this page.

To evaluate, you must give reasons why some people would agree with each statement, and reasons why others would disagree. You should then weigh up the evidence to assess which case is the stronger, and then state your own point of view.

This paves the way for explanations of the Buddha's teachings about the nature of life:

> All conditioned things are transient (anicca). All conditioned things are sorrowful (dukkha). All Dhammas are without a soul (anatta). When one understands this with wisdom, one is disgusted with suffering. This is the path to purity. (277–279)
>
> The one who has gone for refuge to the Buddha, the Dhamma and the Sangha sees with the right knowledge the Four Noble Truths – Suffering, the Cause of Suffering, the Overcoming of Suffering, and the End of Suffering – which are led by the Noble Eightfold Path. This is indeed secure refuge. This is indeed supreme refuge. By seeking such refuge, one is released from all suffering. (190–192)

Finally, the Dhammapada describes the aim of following the path – buddhahood:

> For those who have completed the journey, left sorrow behind, being completely free from everything and destroyed all attachment, the fever of passion does not exist. (90)
>
> The sun shines by day; the moon is radiant by night. The warrior shines in his armour; the Brahmin shines in his meditation. But the Buddha shines in glory all day and night. (387)
>
> By what worldly path could you track down the Buddha, who, enjoying all, can go through the pathless ways of infinite range? The Buddha is the one whose conquest (of passion) is not turned into defeat, and whom no one can conquer. (179)

Since so much of the Dhammapada contains models of worldly wisdom that can be appreciated by anyone, the book is popular with both Buddhist and non-Buddhist alike.

Jataka

The **Jataka** (which means 'Lives (of the Buddha)') consists of 547 stories about previous lives of the Buddha, as both human and animal. They are presented as if it is the Buddha who is telling them. At the end of each he identifies which role he played.

Tradition has it that the stories were taught by the Buddha himself, and became part of the Pali Canon at the meeting of the First Council of the Sangha in 483 BCE. It is more likely, however, that many of them were popular in India before Siddattha's time. They have certainly travelled away from their Indian and religious roots, and are found in Persian, Greek and Jewish cultures, among others. Some even came across to England, where they can be found in the stories of Chaucer.

The Jataka stories are moral tales about developing human values and the qualities of generosity (dana), loving kindness (metta) and wisdom (pranna). By reading the stories, the reader is supposed to relate these qualities to his or her own life. Still today, Buddhist parents read the stories to their children, and they are taught in schools to provide examples of good behaviour.

Here is an example:

> Once upon a time there was a herd of forest deer. In the herd was a wise old stag, looked up to by all the others. He would teach them all he knew about how to survive in the forest.
>
> One day his younger sister brought her son to him and said, 'My young son will soon be old enough to fend for himself. Will you teach him the ways of survival for a deer?' The old stag agreed, and the young deer started to attend classes each day.
>
> After a week, however, he got bored with his lessons, and preferred to go off and play with the other young deer. One day, however, he stepped into a snare and was trapped. When he did not come home, his mother became worried and went to see the old stag. 'Is my son with you?' she asked.
>
> The teacher replied, 'I have not seen him for several days. I tried to teach him, but he was disobedient and stopped coming to his lessons.'
>
> Later, they learned the sad news. The young deer had been trapped by a hunter, killed and butchered.
>
> The moral is: no matter how good the teacher, nothing will be learned by one who does not listen.
>
> *Jataka 15*

Some stories can be understood on a number of levels, like the one on the page opposite:

Long, long ago, a priest decided to offer a sacrifice and bought a goat for that purpose. He said to his students, 'Take this goat, prepare it for sacrifice, then bring it back'.

While they were grooming it, the goat started to laugh. Then, just as strangely, it started to weep loudly.

The young students were amazed. 'Why did you suddenly laugh', they asked the goat, 'and why do you now cry so loudly?'

'Repeat your question when we get back to your teacher', the goat answered.

The students hurriedly took the goat back to their master and told him what had happened. Hearing the story, the master himself asked the goat why it had laughed and why it had wept.

'In a past life, Priest', the goat began, 'I was a priest like you. I, too, sacrificed a goat. Because of killing that single goat, I was reborn as a goat and I have had my head cut off 499 times. I laughed aloud when I realised that this is my last birth as an animal to be sacrificed. Today I will be free. On the other hand, I cried when I realised that, because of killing me, you, too, will be doomed to lose your head 500 times. It was out of pity for you that I cried'.

'Well, goat', said the Priest, 'in that case, I am not going to kill you'.

'Priest!' exclaimed the goat. 'Whether or not you kill me, I cannot escape death today'.

'Don't worry', the priest assured the goat. 'I will guard you'.

'You don't understand', the goat told him. 'Your protection is weak. The force of my evil deed is very strong'.

The priest untied the goat and said to his students, 'Don't allow anyone to harm this goat'. They followed the animal to protect it.

After the goat was freed, it began to graze. It stretched out its neck to reach the leaves on a bush growing near the top of a large rock. At that instant a lightning bolt hit the rock, breaking off a sharp piece of stone, which flew through the air and cut off the goat's head. A crowd of people gathered around the dead goat and began to talk excitedly about the amazing accident.

A tree god had seen everything, and drawing a lesson from the incident, warned the crowd: 'If people only knew that the penalty would be rebirth into sorrow, they would not take life'. The people were so frightened that they completely gave up the practice of animal sacrifices. The god further instructed the people in the Precepts and urged them to do good.

Eventually, that god passed away. For several generations after that, people remained faithful to the Precepts and spent their lives doing good, so that many were reborn in the heavens.

The Buddha ended his lesson and identified himself by saying, 'In those days I was that god'.

Jataka 18

From this story, young children might be taught about the importance of being kind to animals. Older ones may be taught about false religious practices. On the other hand, it may stimulate a discussion on the nature of compassion (karuna) and kamma: should the priest be prepared to be reborn as a goat in order to let the goat be reborn as a human being?

TEST YOURSELF

1 How many sayings are there in the Dhammapada?
2 Why is the Dhammapada popular among non-Buddhists?
3 What are the Jataka tales about?
4 Why are the Jataka read to children?

 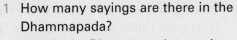

WHY IS THE ABHIDHAMMA IMPORTANT TO BUDDHISTS?

The Vinaya Pitaka and the Sutta Pitaka together give a complete account of the discipline and practice of the path to Buddhahood. The third Pitaka, the Abhidhamma, is very different. Its purpose is to present a painstaking analysis of Buddhist principles. It is an immense work that covers in detail what we would call today human psychology.

In the Abhidhamma, everything is classified, then sub-classified until it is broken down into its smallest components. For example, we have seen (Unit Two, p. 15) that Buddhism says that the human being is made up of five parts, or Khandhas. In the Abhidhamma, each of the Khandhas is subdivided: the physical form has been analysed into 28 constituents; sensation into five; perception into six; the mental formation into 50 and consciousness into 89. Each part is then analysed further in terms of its relationship with each other part.

The Abhidhamma is very difficult to read and very difficult to understand. Yet Buddhists throughout history have shown tremendous respect for it. By way of example, the tenth-century Sri Lankan King Kassapa V had the whole Abhidhamma Pitaka inscribed on gold plates and the first book of it set in gems. The reason why the Abhidhamma is valued so highly is that it is an attempt to describe the whole of life in the minutest detail. For Buddhists, it is not just a theory about life: it is a true picture of reality expressed by an enlightened being.

The Abhidhamma Pitaka is divided into seven books:

1. Dhammasangani (Enumeration of Phenomena) This book enumerates all the paramattha Dhammas (ultimate realities) to be found in the universe.
2. Vibhanga (The Book of Treatises) This book continues the analysis of the Dhammasangani, here in the form of questions and answers.
3. Dhatukatha (Discussion with Reference to the Elements) An examination of the elements of existence.
4. Puggalapaññatti (Description of Individuals) This book contains descriptions of a number of personality types.
5. Kathavatthu (Points of Controversy) An attempt to clarify points of controversy that existed between the various schools of Buddhism at the time.
6. Yamaka (The Book of Pairs) This book is a logical analysis of many concepts presented in the earlier books.
7. Patthana (The Book of Relations) This book, at over 6000 pages long, is by far the longest volume in the Tipitaka. It describes the 24 paccayas that link the Dhammas outlined in the Dhammasangani.

TEST YOURSELF

1 What is the purpose of the Abhidhamma?
2 Why is the Abhidhamma important to Buddhists?

WHICH OTHER BOOKS ARE IMPORTANT TO THERAVADA BUDDHISTS?

Milinda Panha, or the Questions of King Milinda, is not in the Pali Canon, yet is very popular with Theravada Buddhists. It describes a discussion between the Indian bhikkhu, Nagasena, and the Greek King Milinda. Milinda wants to learn about Buddhism, and so asks Nagasena 237 questions. In answering them, Nagasena presents the Buddhist Dhamma in a way that can be easily understood. In the course of the discussions, Milinda asks most of the questions that many a non-Buddhist would ask, such as:

- 'Did the Buddha really exist?'
- 'Why do some people live a long time and others die young?'
- 'Where is kamma stored?'

- 'If Nibbana means giving up all attachments, how can it be a perfectly happy state?'
- 'If there is no fixed self (anatta), then who am I talking to?'

Read the examples of King Milinda's questions given on these pages. How would you answer them if you were Nagasena?

You should be able to answer all of them using information from previous Units.

In the following example, King Milinda and Nagasena are discussing rebirth in Samsara:

'When a person is reborn, Nagasena, is he the same person or another?'

'He is neither the same nor another.'

'Give me an illustration.'

'If milk is left, it turns into curds, which turn into butter, which turns into ghee (clarified butter). It would not be right to say that the curds, the butter and the ghee are the same as the milk, though they have come from it. And since they have come from it, it would not be right to say that they are different.'

Here, the King asks Nagasena how someone can understand what it is like to have attained Nibbana:

'Can a person who has not attained Nibbana understand what it is like?'

'Yes, indeed, O King. Just as those who have not had their hands and feet cut off know that it is painful; so those who have not attained Nibbana can know that it is a state of bliss.'

WHICH WRITINGS ARE SPECIAL FOR MAHAYANA BUDDHISTS?

Although the Theravada collection of scriptures varies slightly from country to country, there is a general agreement about the contents of the Tipitaka. However, because there are so many Mahayana sects throughout the Far East, there is no single Mahayana collection. Most Mahayana sects took on some of the Vinaya and some of the Suttas from the Pali Canon, but a lot was changed and added to, particularly the Abhidhamma.

The **Sutras** (the Sanskrit form of Sutta) are the most important addition to the Mahayana collection of writings. Although they tend to follow the same style as the Theravada Suttas in the way they are written, their focus is very different. Whereas the Theravada Suttas are presented as the teachings of the historical Buddha, the Mahayana Sutras are more mystical and other-worldly.

Some of the most important Mahayana Sutras are:

- The Lotus Sutra.
- The Heart Sutra.
- The Diamond Sutra.
- The Amitabha Sutras.

The Lotus Sutra

▲ Ancient copies of the Sutras can be highly decorated. Writing out and illustrating Buddhist writing is thought to bring good fortune (karma).

The Lotus Sutra was originally written in the Sanskrit language. Its Sanskrit name is Saddharma Pundarika Sutra, which means 'Sutra of the White Lotus of the Universal Law (Dharma)'. We have already seen that the lotus flower is a powerful symbol for Buddhists. Because the large, pure, white, beautiful flower grows from dirty, muddy waters, it shows that everyone, regardless of who they are or what their karma is, can become enlightened. The Sutra was translated several times into Chinese in the third to fifth centuries CE, and its Chinese title is Myoho Renge Kyo. Today, most English versions of the Lotus Sutra are translations from the Chinese.

The Lotus Sutra starts in the same way as the Theravada Suttas, with the words, 'Thus I heard.' It then goes on to describe the circumstances in which the Buddha was teaching. But the circumstances are quite unlike those described in Theravada Suttas. The Buddha is portrayed as a superhuman, universal Buddha, whose nature all human beings share. This is very different message from that of the Theravada Suttas, which say that the Buddha was an ordinary man, that only a few monks can become Arahants, and that there can only be one Buddha at a time.

Furthermore, the world the Buddha teaches in is the sort of world found in science fiction or fantasy books. The Buddha teaches on Vulture Peak. Although Vulture Peak was (and is) a real place where the Buddha would retire to meditate, it is shown in the Lotus Sutra to be a spiritual place, removed from the ordinary world, but coming out of it.

The Buddha is surrounded by 12,000 Arhats, those who have reached Nirvana. There are 80,000 Bodhisattvas, and also tens of thousands of gods and other non-human beings with their attendants. The Buddha teaches about infinity, and so deep and powerful is his teaching that flowers of many colours start raining down from the heavens, and the whole universe trembles. Then the Buddha enters into deep meditation, and a brilliant ray of pure white light shines from a spot between his eyebrows like a great

▲ The Buddha preaching from Vulture Peak. In the Lotus Sutra, the Buddha is portrayed as a superhuman, universal Buddha.

searchlight. It sweeps the universe so that it is possible to see into the depths of space. In that intense light innumerable world systems are discovered. And in every world there is a Buddha preaching, surrounded by disciples, and Bodhisattvas.

This is just the introduction. The scene is set for the Buddha's greatest teaching: the Lotus Sutra. The Sutra uses all sorts of fantastic imagery to get across its message. The message is that buddhahood is the basis of human nature: all humans share the enlightened nature of the universal Buddha, but they do not realise it. It is like a jewel, hidden and unknown to its owner. Revealing the glory and beauty of it is simply a matter of finding it and polishing it. Everyone is capable of becoming a buddha.

The Lotus Sutra is thought by many Mahayana Buddhists to represent the highest point of the Buddha's teaching. The Chinese T'ien T'ai sect uses it as the basis of its beliefs, as do the Nichiren sects of Japan.

Nichiren was a Japanese Tendai (T'ien T'ai) priest in the thirteenth century. His studies of the Lotus Sutra led him to believe that not only was it the greatest of all Buddhist teachings, but that it was the only Buddhist teaching that could lead people to enlightenment. In fact, he claimed that simply chanting its title, Nam Myoho Renge Kyo, brings benefits and protection. It can also draw out a person's enlightened nature: it can make you a buddha. Today, most Buddhists in Japan follow Nichiren's teachings.

The Heart Sutra

The Heart Sutra is one of a collection of Sutras that are together known as the **Prajna** Paramita Sutras. 'Prajna Paramita' means the 'Perfection of Wisdom'. The Heart Sutra is very short, being just over 40 lines long. Yet it contains one of the most important of Mahayana beliefs: **sunyata**.

▲ **The beginning of the Heart Sutra in Sanskrit.**

The message of the Heart Sutra is contained in just three lines of it:

Form is not different from emptiness
And emptiness is not different from form.
Form is emptiness, and emptiness is form.

'Form' means 'stuff', 'physical or material things'. The word used for emptiness is 'sunyata'. So, the three lines mean that physical things are sunya (empty).

We have seen that Buddhists believe that physical things have no fixed or permanent self. The word 'bicycle' is just a label we apply to a mixture of wheels, brakes, gears, handlebars, and so on. A human is a mixture of Five Khandhas (p. 15). Does this mean that the bicycle does not exist? Or the human? The Heart Sutra says, 'Yes and no'. Certainly, the bicycle does not exist as an independent object, but, on the other hand, we cannot say that there is nothing there.

So, the Heart Sutra teaches that 'form' has neither existence nor non-existence. It is just sunya: empty. Now, this means that there is nothing for us to cling to, nothing to tie us down. The fact that everything is sunya means that we can be free. And freedom, for a Buddhist, is enlightenment. Understanding this is called 'Prajna Paramita': the Perfection of Wisdom. Wisdom is the realisation that everything is sunya. This is how the Heart Sutra puts it:

> The Buddhas of past, present and future
> By relying on Prajna Paramita (the wisdom that everything is empty)
> Have attained Supreme Enlightenment.

The Diamond Sutra

The Diamond Sutra is the second most popular of the Prajna Paramita Sutras after the Heart Sutra. Its Sanskrit name is Vajra Cchedika Prajna Paramita Sutra, which means the 'Sutra on the Perfection of Wisdom that Cuts Like a Diamond'. The title is significant. The diamond is known to be the hardest substance on earth: it can cut through anything, yet is itself indestructible and lasts forever. It reflects light and is able, then, to light up darkness.

For Buddhists, the diamond represents **prajna**: wisdom. This wisdom cuts through illusion, breaks up ignorance and is the eternal truth. It is the wisdom of sunyata: emptiness.

The Diamond Sutra takes the form of a dialogue between the Buddha and one of his disciples, Sabhuti. Here is an extract:

> The Buddha told Subhuti, 'All Bodhisattvas should ... vow, "I must cause all living beings ... to enter Nirvana without exception ... Yet of the immeasurable, boundless numbers of living beings led to Nirvana, there is actually no living being led to Nirvana. And why? Subhuti, if a Bodhisattva holds on to an idea of self, of others, of individual identity, or of lifespan, he is not a Bodhisattva."'

Diamond Sutra 3

The Bodhisattva, in delaying his or her own enlightenment in order to lead others to it, represents compassion (karuna): the ability to feel the suffering of others as one's own. True karuna means feeling so deeply for others that you become one with them. Then you realise that you have no individual identity, and nor do they. You all share the same identity, the same life. True compassion, therefore, involves realising anatta (no fixed self), and that the nature of anatta is sunyata (emptiness).

A Bodhisattva who sees a distinction between himself and those he is trying to help is attached to them. His tanha (desire) is the want to help them. He has tanha because he believes he has an individual identity, a self (atman), which is an illusion. He is therefore tied to ignorance. The realisation of the sunya (empty) nature of things cuts through the ignorance, like a diamond, revealing enlightenment. Ignorance is the obstacle to enlightenment.

The Diamond Sutra, along with the Heart Sutra, is one of the most popular of the Mahayana texts. It is a short work, having 32 sections that can be recited in about 40 minutes. It is therefore popular for chanting. It is also used as a subject for study by those who wish to reveal their own enlightenment.

TEST YOURSELF

1 How do Mahayana Sutras differ from Theravada Suttas?
2 What is the message of the Lotus Sutra?
3 Describe what the Heart Sutra teaches about sunyata.
4 Why is the Diamond Sutra so-called?

WHICH WRITINGS ARE SPECIAL FOR TIBETAN BUDDHISTS?

Tibetan Buddhism grew out of the Mahayana tradition, so it inherited the Mahayana canon. Some of the Vinaya (rules for monks and nuns) was adapted to suit Tibetan culture, but the Mahayana Sutras were accepted as they were. To these were added the **Tantra**, volumes of mystical literature, which can be very difficult to understand for someone who is not trained. The Tibetan collection of Vinaya, Sutras and Tantra is called Kanjur. In addition, there are hundreds of volumes of Abhidharma and writings about the Sutras, called Tanjur.

Bardo Thodol

One of the most famous Tibetan writings is called Bardo Thodol. In English it is usually called the Tibetan Book of the Dead, but its proper title is The Great Liberation upon Hearing in the Intermediate State. Although it is not actually in the Tibetan canon, it is very popular, especially in the West. The Tibetan Book of the Dead is a book of advice given to someone who is dying. It explains the various stages through which he or she will go before taking on another life. The time between one life and the next is called the Bardo ('Bardo' means 'between'). Traditionally, this may take just a moment, or as long as 49 days.

The book describes various phases that you go through during this period. They are dream-like states in which you are given various choices. What you choose depends on the karma you have created by the actions you made in your life, but it also determines what sort of life you will lead in the future. In this way your own deeds and attitudes lead you to choose another life.

▲ Images of the Bardo are fantastical and frightening.

At the moment of death you enter the First Bardo. You are met by a clear, bright light. It is the Light of the Ultimate Reality, which is truth and wisdom. If you recognise it and respond accordingly, you will be taken into the spirit of the Buddha forever. Most do not recognise it, and descend to the Second Bardo.

The Second Bardo is a place of wonder and terror. It is a place where you hear colours and see sounds. During the first week in this Bardo, you are met by various peaceful gods. If you have good karma, the meetings are joyous; if not, they are fearful. In the second week, you are met by angry gods. They drink blood from human skulls and threaten horrible torture. Actually, they are the peaceful gods in disguise. If you recognise this, then you are saved; if not, the Third Bardo awaits.

In the Third Bardo, you encounter the Lord of Death. He appears in smoke and fire, holding up the Mirror of Karma. You are faced with everything you have done in your life, and the Lord of Death punishes you for all the bad things. He will put a rope around your neck and drag you, cut off your head, pull out your heart and your intestines, lick up your brain, drink your blood, eat your flesh and gnaw your bones. But you will not die: you are dead already. So you will have to put up with this treatment time after time. Just hope that you do not catch him when he is in a bad mood! If you are able to recognise that the Lord of Death is empty (sunya), then you will be saved. If not, then you will have to face another lifetime in Samsara.

You are still petrified as you leave the Third Bardo, and desperate to find somewhere to hide. You find a cave and crawl into it for safety. But it is not a cave: it is your mother's womb.

The final part of the Tibetan Book of the Dead gives advice on how to choose the best 'cave' for a fortunate rebirth: 'Let virtue and goodness be perfected in every way.'

The book is studied by people who may be close to death to help them prepare for the Bardo and rebirth. It is read to dying people, usually by a lama or a friend, who is taught to recognise the signs and symptoms of death. It is read as soon as death has occurred, and then on the 49th day afterwards.

TASK BOX

a) Describe what Buddhists believe about death and life after death.

Use information from this Unit and Unit One to answer this question.

b) Why do you think the Tibetan Book of the Dead is so popular in the West?

c) What might the Tibetan Book of the Dead teach the living?

TEST YOURSELF

1 What English names are given to the Bardo Thodol?
2 What is the Bardo Thodol about?
3 What is a Bardo?
4 How is the Bardo Thodol used in Tibetan culture?

http://www.accesstoinsight.org/canon/ *A sizeable collection of English translations of some of the Tipitaka.*

http://www.buddhanet.net/e-learning/history/s_theracanon.htm *A chart displaying the contents of the Tipitaka.*

http://www.buddhanet.net/e-learning/history/s_mahasutras.htm *A table describing the important Mahayana Sutras.*

http://www.buddhanet.net/e-learning/history/s_tibcanon.htm *An outline of the Tibetan canon.*

http://www.accesstoinsight.org/canon/vinaya/bhikkhu-pati.html *The complete list of Patimokkha rules for bhikkhus.*

http://www.accesstoinsight.org/canon/vinaya/bhikkhuni-pati.html *The complete list of Patimokkha rules for bhikkhunis.*

http://ignca.nic.in/jatak.htm *A large collection of illustrated Jataka stories, together with other stories about the Buddha.*

http://www.buddhanet.net/monkey1.htm *A cartoon version of one of the tales.*

http://www.sgi-usa.org/buddhism/library/Buddhism/LotusSutra/ *A very accurate translation of the Lotus Sutra.*

http://www.silcom.com/~eclarson/heartsutra/hs-ra/hs01.html *Contains an audio file of the Heart Sutra being chanted in Tibetan.*

http://www.hm.tyg.jp/~acmuller/bud-canon/diamond_sutra.html *An English translation of the Diamond Sutra.*

http://www.himalayanart.org/search/set.cfm?setID=227 *Thankas of Bardo gods.*

http://alexm.here.ru/mirrors/www.enteract.com/jwalz/Eliade/162.html *An English translation of the first part of the Tibetan Book of the Dead.*

WEBLINKS

REMEMBER

> ▸ The Pali canon of Theravada Buddhism is called the Tipitaka.
> ▸ Tipitaka means 'Three Baskets'.
> ▸ The Vinaya Pitaka contains rules of discipline for bhikkhus.
> ▸ The Sutta Pitaka contains the Buddha's teachings.
> ▸ The Abhidhamma Pitaka contains commentaries on the teachings.
> ▸ A Sutta is a teaching from the Theravadin canon.
> ▸ A Sutra is a teaching from the Mahayana or Vajrayana canon.

1 a) Describe the contents of the Tipitaka. (8 marks)

b) Explain how Buddhists might use the teachings from their scriptures in their daily lives. (7 marks)

c) 'Reading the Suttas will not make you enlightened.'

Do you agree? Give reasons for your answer, showing that you have thought about more than one point of view. (5 marks)

2 a) Describe the themes of the Prajna Paramita Sutras. (8 marks)

b) Explain how the Bardo Thodol is used in Tibetan Buddhism. (6 marks)

c) 'The Tipitaka is useless if the Buddha did not write it.'

Do you agree? Give reasons for your opinion, showing that you have thought about different points of view. (4 marks)

Assignment

7

KEY WORDS

Ahimsa: 'Not harming', non-violence.

Dana: 'Generosity'.

Engaged Buddhism: The use of Buddhism to help people by engaging mindfulness.

Karuna: 'Compassion', sharing in the sufferings of others.

Kshanti: 'Patience'.

Metta: 'Loving kindness'.

Pansil: The Five Precepts (short for Pancha Sila).

Prajna: 'Wisdom'.

Samadhi: State of deep meditation.

Sila: 'Morality'.

Upaya kausala: 'Skilful means'.

Virya: 'Energy'.

WHY IS IT IMPORTANT FOR BUDDHISTS TO DO GOOD?

KEY QUESTION

How do Buddhists make moral decisions?

The law of kamma, at its most basic level, means that Buddhists attempt to live moral lives. Doing good will create merit and help a person on the path to Nibbana. So, for a Buddhist, moral behaviour is an important part of his or her spiritual journey. The Dhammapada says, 'Do not do any evil. Cultivate good. Purify your mind – this is the teaching of the Buddha' (183). In a way, this quotation is a summary of Buddhism. It says that enlightenment depends partly on moral behaviour.

We have seen, in any case, that Buddhism teaches anatta: that there is no fixed self, that things are 'conditioned' – they exist only in relation to, and because of, other things. It could be said that people do not have individual lives; they share the same life. Therefore, working for the welfare of others is the same as working for your own welfare.

So, Buddhists attempt to lead good lives for the benefit of all beings, which includes themselves.

How do Buddhists decide what is right and wrong?

The simple answer to this question is: any thought, speech or action that is motivated by greed, hatred or stupidity (the Three Poisons) is wrong; thoughts, words and actions that are motivated by generosity, love or wisdom are right. What is important here is motivation: your intention rather than the end result. Most people would agree that deliberately driving an axe through somebody's skull is worse, morally, than accidentally running over a person who appears suddenly from behind a parked car. The end results are identical: the death of an individual. What is different is the intention. Buddhists try to be mindful not only of the effects that their actions have on other people, but also whether their intentions are pure.

Buddhists, therefore, see leading a moral life as entailing two things. First, it means cultivating the qualities and attitudes that encourage positive relationships between people. These are, most importantly, **metta** (loving kindness), **karuna** (compassion), and the six qualities known as the Paramitas. Secondly, it means following guidelines on how to behave in a way that supports others and helps create positive kamma. This means keeping to the Five Precepts and other teachings from the Suttas.

METTA

We have seen that in avoiding violence and causing harm to others, Buddhists try to develop loving kindness. They call this 'metta'. Metta is a universal love for all beings. All beings respond well to metta: humans, animals and even plants. Buddhists try to cultivate an awareness of the effects that anger and hatred have on others. At the same time, they try to become aware of the positive effects that love, care and warmth have.

Metta is not only beneficial to others. The Suttas say that there are 11 personal benefits of practising it: peaceful sleep, waking with a clear mind, no bad dreams, kindness to people, kindness to animals, admiration, protection, concentration, a bright complexion, a peaceful death and a fortunate rebirth. In the Metta Sutta, the Buddha explained the nature of love in Buddhism. 'Just as a mother would protect her only child even at the risk of her own life, even so, let him cultivate a boundless heart towards all beings. Let his thoughts of boundless love pervade the whole world, above, below and across without any obstruction, without any hatred, without any enmity.' If the number of lives you have had is infinite, then every other person at some time has been your mother, and you have been a mother to everyone else. Metta means treating people as if that were the case.

KARUNA

After Siddattha Gotama became enlightened, he had to decide whether to keep his knowledge about life to himself, or whether to teach it to others so that they, too, could become enlightened. The Suttas say that the choice was a difficult one. He was not sure whether all people would be able to understand his teachings. He realised that for them to understand and follow the Dhamma would mean giving up their faith in God and belief in a soul. He knew that this would be difficult for most people to do.

It is said that Brahma Sahampati, a Hindu deity, saw the Buddha's indecision, and left Heaven to convince him to preach the Dhamma. He said:

> You are no longer Siddattha Gotama; you are Buddha. You are the Blessed One who is blessed with the fullest enlightenment. You are the Tathagatha (the Thus Come One). How can you refuse to enlighten the world? How can you refuse to save erring humanity? There are beings full of impurity that are falling away through not hearing the teachings ... May the Lord in his compassion agree to teach the Dhamma to all people.

▲ Our life-state has an enormous effect on those around us.

▲ After his enlightenment, the Buddha was reluctant to teach the Dhamma to others. It was his compassion (karuna) that motivated him to do it.

Knowing that there was so much unhappiness in the world, the Buddha realised that he could not keep his understanding of the Dhamma to himself and allow things to remain as they were. He had found asceticism to be useless. It was unrealistic to attempt to escape from the world. There is no escape from the world even for an ascetic. He realised that what was necessary was not to escape from the world. What was necessary was to change people's view of the world; to take them out of ignorance.

If he could drive misery and unhappiness from the world by spreading his teaching, it was his duty to be part of the world and serve it, and not sit silently and impassively.

The Buddha therefore agreed to the request of Brahma Sahampati and decided to preach the Dhamma to the world.

It was his compassion for the sufferings of ordinary people that finally persuaded the Buddha to teach the Dhamma. Buddhists call this compassion 'karuna'.

TASK BOX

Explain how Brahma Sahampati convinced the Buddha to preach the Dhamma.

What arguments did he use?

Why was the Buddha persuaded?

Karuna does not mean feeling sorry for people. Feeling sorry for someone, however well intentioned, can be patronising because it comes from a position of emotional superiority. Karuna means feeling the suffering of others as your own, and recognising that you cannot be truly happy so long as there are people who are not.

Karuna can be active, helping people who are distressed mentally, emotionally or physically. But it is, above all, a frame of mind, an attitude to others that motivates all of your actions. It is a state of concern for all beings, and a desire to relieve them of their troubles.

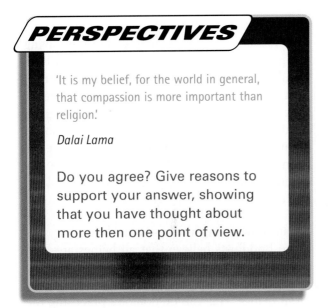

'It is my belief, for the world in general, that compassion is more important than religion.'

Dalai Lama

Do you agree? Give reasons to support your answer, showing that you have thought about more then one point of view.

THE PARAMITAS

The Six Paramitas – or Perfections – are the qualities of an enlightened mind. These are the qualities a person needs to develop if he or she is going to make progress towards enlightenment.

■ Dana (generosity)   A person who is generous shows that he or she has overcome attachments, is not grasping and craving for money or other goods, but is happy to let them go for the benefit of others. Generosity, of course, is not just a matter of giving money, but also of giving time, support or skills for the benefit of others. In some parts of the Buddhist world, **dana** is expressed especially in supporting those who are monks and nuns, so that they can be free from the need to earn a living, and can devote themselves to practising and teaching the Dhamma.

■ Sila (morality)   **Sila** means not just moral behaviour, but also being a moral person. It is often the case that we do wrong, but persuade ourselves that it is right. We justify bad behaviour. So sila means being honest with yourself, and recognising your actions for what they are, right or wrong. To develop sila means developing the predisposition to do good.

■ Virya (energy)   It is not enough to think positive thoughts. Buddhists need to take action in order to get things done. Showing loving kindness towards all creatures is not easy, nor is it much use if it is only a nice feeling. The Buddhist path may need carefully directed effort. Meditation can help with this: people find they have more energy if their minds are focused. **Virya** is the name Buddhists give to the energy that is directed towards doing good.

■ Kshanti (patience)   **Kshanti** does not mean always giving way to what other people want, but behaving in a thoughtful way, recognising each person's individual abilities and needs. You can only be patient with other people when you are patient with yourself – when you accept and understand your own abilities and limitations.

▲ The Six Paramitas are sometimes represented symbolically as six types of animal surrounding the Buddha: Lions (wisdom), Elephants (meditation), Dwarves (energy), Makaras – a cross between a crocodile and a hippopotamus – (patience), Nagas – a dragon-serpent – (morality), Garuda – a cross between a man and an eagle – (generosity).

- Samadhi (meditation)   We saw in Unit Five that meditation is important for the Buddhist way of life. If a person's mind is always rushing from one thought to the next, he or she is unlikely to be able to stand back and see life calmly, or to recognise what are the most important things. **Samadhi** is a state of deep meditation.

- Prajna (wisdom)   The basic teachings of the Buddha, especially the Three Universal Truths, describe life as it is. Everything changes and has no permanent identity, so life inevitably involves suffering. The nature of things is sunyata (emptiness). **Prajna** means accepting these ideas as truths and responding to them in a skilful and appropriate way.

TEST YOURSELF

1 Why is intention important in evaluating moral behaviour?
2 What is metta?
3 How can your metta for others benefit you?
4 Why are the Six Paramitas important for Buddhists?

THE FIVE PRECEPTS (PANSIL)

We have seen (pp. 18–19) that the Noble Eightfold Path gives specific guidelines on developing the Paramita of sila (morality). These guidelines are contained within Right Speech, Right Action and Right Livelihood. Right Action, in particular, provides a code of moral behaviour in the form of Five Precepts. In Pali, the Five Precepts are known as Pancha Sila ('five moral principles'), and this is often shortened to **Pansil**.

There are two ways of looking at the Precepts. The more usual way is to see them as a list of things to be avoided. They all start with the words, 'I undertake to abstain from …', which means, 'I promise to myself that I shall avoid …' On the other hand, it is equally possible to list them in terms of positive qualities that a person should develop. Here we have the negative form followed by the positive.

1. I undertake to abstain from taking life.
This Precept is against killing or harming living things – including animals. Ideally, Buddhists should therefore be vegetarians, but in practice, many are not. Bhikkhus, of course, eat whatever they are given by lay Buddhists. If they are given meat, it would be wasteful and ungrateful not to eat it. Buddhists try to eat organic food that has been humanely killed, wherever possible. By extension, this Precept is against any violent, aggressive or harmful behaviour.

I shall show loving kindness to all beings.
Since Buddhists believe that all beings are connected by sharing life, developing an attitude of loving kindness (metta) increases the happiness of all beings. This can be done by practising the Metta Bhavana meditation (see Unit Five) and by cultivating mindfulness. In this way they will be aware of the effect that they have on other people.

2. I undertake to abstain from taking what is not freely given.
In its simplest form this is a Precept against stealing, but it can be far more than that. You may do something that is quite legal, but which aims to exploit others for your own gain: this would also be against the second Precept. It is not a matter of law, but an attitude that seeks to get what belongs to others, or disrespect what is theirs. Some forms of high-pressure advertising or selling take other people's time and energy, as well as their money.

I shall show generosity to all beings.
This does not just mean giving (though it does mean that). It also means cultivating an attitude of wanting others to do well. Jealousy of what other people have got is very destructive. It not only hurts you, but, if it leads to attempts to get what other people have, it can involve ruthlessness and a disregard for their feelings. The Suttas say that there are five consequences of being generous: you will be very popular, you will have good friends, you will have a good reputation, you will have lots of self-confidence, and you will have a fortunate rebirth.

3. I undertake to refrain from the misuse of the senses.

This Precept is against over-indulgence. In its simplest form it is against sexual misconduct that harms oneself and others. Buddhist monks, nuns and some lay people undertake to live without sex, so that they can follow the spiritual path in an undistracted way. For others, there are no strict rules about how they should express their sexuality. The important thing is that causing harm – either physically or emotionally – or taking advantage of another person sexually, leads to unhappiness and therefore is to be avoided. Some Buddhists extend this Precept to include any form of over-indulgence, for example in food or drink. The Precept is really about being in control of your life, and not being controlled by your desires and attachments.

I shall show respect to all beings.

Sex should be an expression of love and intimacy between two people, and when it is, it contributes to one's mental and emotional well-being. The positive aspect of this Precept also means that you should be responsible and loyal in relationships, and value friendships.

4. I undertake to abstain from wrong speech.

Buddhists should avoid speaking negatively to or about anyone. They therefore avoid lying, slandering, gossiping, speaking harshly or unfairly, and talking about nothing.

I shall show honesty and sincerity to all beings.

This involves being honest with other people and with oneself. It includes not giving the wrong impression, or trying to be someone you are not, but being yourself and sharing your thoughts in a straightforward way. Buddhists should also try to cultivate helpful, gentle and kindly speech.

5. I undertake to abstain from drugs and alcohol that cloud the mind.

Although some Buddhists do drink alcohol, they do so only in moderation, and they do not allow their minds to become fogged and clouded by it. Some people drink to relax and get rid of stress and tension; but Buddhists would say that meditation techniques are more effective and less harmful. Others drink to help them escape from unhappiness; but that is not the Buddhist way, either. Drink and drugs should also be avoided because of what they lead to. The Sigalovada Sutta says that they bring six types of misfortune: loss of one's property, quarrels, sickness, a bad reputation, moral shame and poor mental health. Also, breaking this Precept increases the chances of breaking the other four.

I shall show mindfulness in my actions.

Buddhism is about being 'awake': a buddha is fully awake to the truth of life. You need a clear mind. A person cannot hope to make progress if he or she tries to hide away from the truth by retreating into a drunken haze. One of the purposes of Buddhist meditation is to help a person become more mindful – to be aware of everything that he or she does at every moment, and why; to avoid going through life in a dream.

▲ Pansil is usually chanted by monks at the beginning of puja.

Upaya kausala (skilful means)

The problem with rules is that no two people are exactly the same; what is right for one person may be wrong for another. But the Paramitas and Precepts are not rules, they are pointers to the sort of life that enables people to be healthy, happy individuals.

A wise person, guided by these pointers, will know what to do in each particular situation, but this takes skill rather than simple obedience to a rule. It means tailoring action to the particular circumstances of each individual. For Buddhists, this skill comes from drawing on the Paramitas and applying the wisdom, compassion and courage that come from Buddhist practices like meditation and chanting. The intention behind an action is most important. Buddhists try to develop pure minds to act wisely. This wisdom is called **upaya kausala**.

For this reason, Buddhists speak of actions as skilful or unskilful rather than as good or bad.

TASK BOX

a) Do you believe that what is good or right in one situation must be good or right in all situations?

b) Do you believe that what is good or right for one person has to be good or right for everybody?

Give reasons to support your answers, and refer to the Buddhist principle of upaya kausala.

AHIMSA

▲ Ahimsa is an ancient Indian idea that was developed within Buddhism.

The cultivation of the first Precept, not to kill, is called **ahimsa**. The Dhammapada says, 'All tremble at the rod. Life is dear to all. Comparing others with oneself, one should neither kill nor cause to kill. (129)' Lying behind this is the idea of anatta: no fixed self. We are used to thinking of ourselves being at the centre of our lives, and seeing everyone else as external to us. It is natural, then, to put ourselves before others. Buddhism teaches that, if you get rid of the idea of the self, then you see that all beings are one ('comparing others with oneself'). Then the happiness of all beings is equally important. At the heart of the quotation is the sentence, 'Life is dear to all'.

Ahimsa means 'not harming' or non-violence. It indicates not using aggression towards other living beings. But it also refers to the state of mind in which you see all beings, including yourself,

A New Approach – Buddhism

related to each other; at the same time, you recognise how precious life is. So ahimsa is not just about what you do; it is, above all, about the kind of person you are. You need to be a peaceful person to be confident of acting peacefully. Violence and aggression come out of hatred and anger. Peace comes from a peaceful mind: ahimsa.

TEST YOURSELF

1 Why are the Five Precepts not rules?
2 Where does upaya kausala come from?
3 Why do Buddhists not use moral words like good/bad, right/wrong?
4 Which step of the Noble Eightfold Path do the Five Precepts correspond to?

TASK BOX

Explain how the principles described in this Unit might guide a Buddhist's thinking about the punishment of criminals.

You need to think about what the aims and purposes of punishing wrongdoers are, and then consider what Buddhism would say about each of them. You must, of course, back up your conclusions with evidence.

THE SIGALOVADA SUTTA

▲ The Buddha instructs Sigala in the Five Precepts.

Most of the Buddha's teachings were directed at bhikkhus, but a few were delivered to lay people. They contain advice on how a lay believer can practise the Dhamma while remaining a householder. One such set of teachings was given to Sigala, a householder's son, and is called the Sigalovada Sutta. It contains guidance on how lay people should conduct themselves in various relationships: parents and children, husband and wife, teachers and pupils, and employers and employees. Lay Buddhists today refer to it for direction in these areas.

'If you have a piano on your foot, I should help you to remove it because of your discomfort, not because I hope to improve my own soul, and still less for hope of reward or fear of punishment. It is you that matters, not me. If I am treating you merely as an opportunity to do myself a bit of good in the eyes of the Almighty I am already deficient in sympathy and decency. You try to rescue your children from a burning building because of the children, not because a sacred text commands you to do so.'

Simon Blackburn, Professor of Philosophy, University of Cambridge

What are Professor Blackburn's criticisms of religions?

Do you think that his criticisms apply to Buddhism? Give reasons for your answer, and show that you have thought about other points of view.

HOW DO BUDDHISTS PUT THEIR BELIEFS ABOUT MORAL ISSUES INTO PRACTICE?

On one occasion, the Buddha is said to have refused to preach until a poor, hungry peasant was fed. Buddhism is aimed at overcoming suffering, and should be practical in its attempts to do so. For Buddhists today, taking action to reduce suffering is seen as a religious duty.

Buddhism is sometimes seen as an otherworldly religion, yet, especially in the East, it has been challenging and changing society for 2500 years. From the Emperor Asoka onwards, societies have been influenced by Buddhist values. Here are some modern examples.

■ During the Vietnam War, groups of Buddhists helped to develop local communities in places that had been ravaged by the war. They did not take sides in the conflict, but showed compassion towards those whose lives had been shattered by it.

■ When there was civil unrest in Burma in the 1980s, Buddhist monks used non-violent means to help the political struggle. They organised demonstrations, held the weapons of army deserters in safekeeping, and their monasteries provided safe havens for those whose lives were in danger.

■ The Dalai Lama, the head of the Tibetan people, travels the world talking about Buddhism. But he also talks about the people of Tibet and the suffering of the people under Chinese rule. He meets with political as well as religious leaders. In this sense, he is politically active. He is seen by Tibetans as both a practical and spiritual guide.

Like all religions, there have been times when Buddhism has been more active in changing society, yet there have been others when it has tended to accept the political situation in which it has found itself.

Engaged Buddhism

Buddhist ethics are based on getting rid of the Three Poisons – greed, hatred and ignorance. This can apply on a personal level, but many Buddhists argue that it applies in a wider sense to the institutions that operate in and influence our society. Thinking about the arms industry, or profits made at the expense of people or the environment by multinational corporations, may be a way of seeing how the Three Poisons can operate across the world.

▲ Thich Nhat Hahn.

Thich Nhat Hahn (pronounced Tick-Naught-Han), a Zen Buddhist from Vietnam, speaks of **engaged Buddhism** – Buddhism that is concerned about people and the way they live and which engages in trying to improve life for them. He sees it as a matter of bringing Buddhist values and spiritual qualities into all areas of life. He runs workshops to help people do just that: to develop kindness, to breathe mindfully in all circumstances, to look deeper and to allow compassion to be manifested before acting, and to live in a way that reflects basic Buddhist ethical principles. He was nominated for the Nobel Peace prize by Martin Luther King, Jr, in 1967, and today runs a meditation community at Plum Village in France, www.plumvillage.org.

There are many ways in which Buddhists may be engaged. In Britain, for example, there is the Network of Engaged Buddhists, which is involved in a range of social issues. Buddhists are concerned with those who are dying, with the poor and the homeless, and with those in prison. Through the Karuna Trust, the Friends of the Western Buddhist Order is particularly concerned to help the ex-untouchable Buddhists of India (see p. 139). Soka Gakkai International, a Japan-based Buddhist sect, advises the United Nations on matters concerning peace and disarmament.

The Dalai Lama sometimes speaks of 'universal responsibility'. You can think of it in this way:

- The world has limited resources.
- The world has an increasing population.
- The environment affects everyone, and what we do affects the environment.

In everything we do – choosing how to travel, what we eat, what sort of work we do, how we heat our homes – we have an effect on the rest of the world. Having 'universal responsibility' means taking this into account. A person's actions always have consequences (kamma). The same applies to actions taken by groups of people, organisations or nations. This 'collective' kamma affects everyone, for better or worse.

How do you deal with the world's problems while keeping the sense of peace that Buddhism seeks to offer? When he received his Nobel Peace Prize in 1989, the Dalai Lama said this:

> ... if you have inner peace, the external problems do not affect your deep sense of peace and tranquillity. In that state of mind you can deal with situations with calmness and reason, while keeping your inner happiness.

In other words, there is no conflict between developing inner spiritual qualities and social action. The first provides a secure foundation on which to build the second.

TEST YOURSELF

A B C

1 How can Buddhists put ahimsa into practice?
2 Write a definition of 'engaged Buddhism'.
3 How might a Buddhist justify coming into conflict with others?
4 How do individuals affect the world?

WEBLINKS

🕷 http://www.speakeasy.org/
~tchilders/mgl_html/
precept.html *The Five
Wonderful (positive) Precepts
of Zen Master Thich Nhat
Hanh, with his commentary.*

🕷 http://www.londonbuddhist
vihara.co.uk/veneration.htm
*Audio file of the monks of the
London Buddhist Vihara
chanting Pansil.*

🕷 http://www.dharmanet.org/
engaged.html
*Provides links to sites on
engaged-Buddhist projects.*

🕷 http://www.prajnaparamita.com/
*Information on Thich Nhat Hanh, including
Martin Luther King's letter nominating him
for the Nobel Peace Prize.*

REMEMBER

▷ The Five Precepts are not rules. Buddhists see them as opportunities to move towards compassion and mindfulness.
▷ Upaya Kausala means using wisdom to decide how to act in each situation.
▷ Metta means 'loving kindness'.
▷ Karuna means 'compassion'.
▷ Engaged Buddhists apply Buddhist principles to social action.

---

1 a) Describe in detail the principles that Buddhists use to make moral decisions. (10 marks)
   b) How might cultivating ahimsa bring a Buddhist into conflict with other people? (6 marks)
   c) 'People are not good or bad; they are just skilful or unskilful.'
      Do you agree? Give reasons to support your answer, and show that you have thought about different points of view. You must refer to Buddhism in your answer. (4 marks)

2 a) Describe what Buddhists mean by karuna. (4 marks)
   b) Describe what Buddhists mean by metta. (4 marks)
   c) Explain why the Five Precepts are important for Buddhists. (7 marks)
   d) 'People need rules if they are to behave well.'
      Do you agree? Give reasons for your opinion, showing that you have considered another point of view. In your answer you should refer to Buddhism. (5 marks)

Assignment

UNIT EIGHT | Buddhist Perspectives on Moral Issues

8

KEY WORDS

Abortion: The induced termination of a pregnancy, resulting in the death of the foetus.

Caste: In Indian culture, the social position a person inherits from his or her family.

Conception: The fertilisation of an egg by a sperm resulting in pregnancy.

Discrimination: Unfair or unequal treatment of somebody because of his or her age, sex, race, religion or disability.

Esho funi: The oneness of life with its environment.

Euthanasia: Ending the life of a person with a painful, terminal illness, for the purpose of relieving that person of suffering.

Hospice: A facility or service that provides supportive care for terminally ill patients and their families.

Right Livelihood: The principle that a person's employment should conform to Buddhist ethics.

Sky burial: A traditional Tibetan funeral in which the corpse is exposed to the open air to be eaten by vultures.

HOW DO BUDDHISTS' BELIEFS AFFECT THE WORK THEY DO?

KEY QUESTION

How does Buddhism affect everyday life?

While bhikkhus in the Theravada tradition set themselves aside from the ordinary world, lay Buddhists have to work in order to support themselves and their families. Since a person's work is likely to take up at least half of the waking day, it is very important to choose one's job carefully. Different people have different reasons for choosing particular jobs. Some may be concerned about the rate of pay, some may wish to help people less fortunate than themselves, some may want a job that makes them look important, some may want to work with animals.

For Buddhists, employment is thought to be a significant part of the spiritual journey towards Nibbana. So important is it, in fact, that it is a stage on the Noble Eightfold Path: Right Livelihood (or Right Employment). Right Livelihood is the principle that a Buddhist should not have a job that goes against other Buddhist principles. In practice, this means a job that conforms to the Five Precepts.

A Buddhist would not, therefore, have a job that involved violence or harm to another living being, human or animal. He or she would not earn a living by taking from others that which is not given willingly. Exploiting sex in order to make money would be unacceptable, as would be peddling lies or gossip about people, or trading in alcohol or drugs. The Suttas give five categories of improper occupations: trading in meat (alive or dead), stealing, cheating, working for a bad person and working only for money.

The Suttas give no suggestions as to what would be a good job for a Buddhist to have. It is fair, though, to assume that a good job would conform to the positive side of the Five Precepts. So a Buddhist is likely to seek a job that helps others, contributes to their well-being, respects their dignity, is honest and encourages thoughtfulness.

The Sigalovada Sutta gives advice for both employer and employee. It says that the employer has a duty to ensure that the work suits the employee's ability, that wages should be fair, that there should be sickness benefits, that employees should share in any profits, and that adequate leave should be given. In return, employees should work longer hours than their employers, be satisfied with their wages, work to the best of their ability, and uphold the reputation of the business.

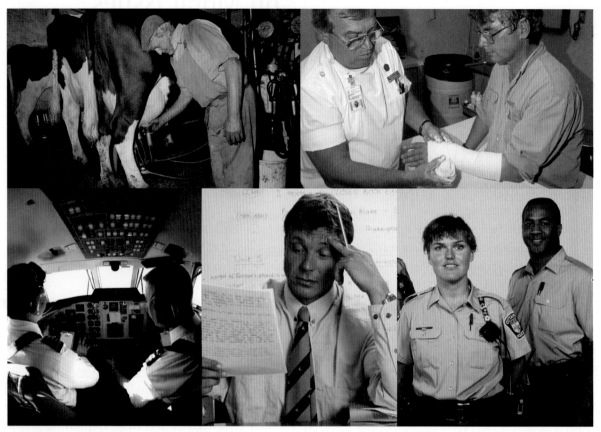

▲ What makes people do the jobs they do?

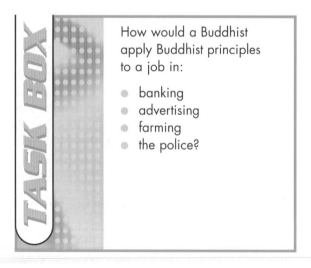

How would a Buddhist apply Buddhist principles to a job in:

- banking
- advertising
- farming
- the police?

TASK BOX

Belief in action: Right Livelihood

Various Buddhist groups throughout the world have attempted to apply the principle of **Right Livelihood** to the work that they do. In Europe, the Friends of the Western Buddhist Order (FWBO) has created Right Livelihood businesses. These are team-based, team-led and team-run organisations that enable individuals to use their work as part of their spiritual practice.

The businesses that the FWBO has set up are ethical businesses. This means that they produce and promote products that do no harm to people or the environment. At the same time, they try to work for the benefit of the world. Some of the businesses are wholefood shops and vegetarian restaurants. Wages are paid according to the needs of the workers. Those who have personal responsibilities for others, for example, will be paid more than those who do not. Any profits that the businesses make go to support FWBO projects, which include charitable works.

A New Approach – Buddhism

HOW DO BUDDHIST BELIEFS AFFECT FAMILY RELATIONSHIPS?

Buddhism takes the view that marriage is a social institution, a legal contract that binds a man and woman together. It is not a religious matter. In spite of that, the Buddha gave advice and guidance on how married couples could live happily. The Sigalovada Sutta outlines five duties that a husband has towards his wife. They are:

■ To be kind to her.
■ To respect her.
■ To be faithful to her.
■ To share responsibilities with her.
■ To provide for her needs.

At the same time, it specifies a wife's duties to her husband:

■ To look after the house well.
■ To provide hospitality for guests.
■ To be faithful.
■ To be careful with the household budget.
■ To work hard at her duties.

Since Buddhists do not consider marriage to have a religious significance, there is no obligation for them to get married. Therefore, Buddhists have no religious objection to a couple living together without being married. What is important for them is the quality of the relationship, not its legal status. The quality of the relationship depends upon the deep respect a couple has for each other. They can be guided in their relationship by the Five Precepts. Each partner has a responsibility to follow the Precepts. This means that:

■ They should not cause suffering to one another, either physically or emotionally.
■ They should be prepared to compromise, to share in the relationship.
■ They should express their love for each other, not force themselves on the other, and not have affairs.
■ They should be honest and truthful.
■ They should keep their emotions pure and wholesome.

If a couple does decide to get married, they may wish to have their marriage blessed at a Buddhist ceremony. For obvious reasons, there is no fixed wedding service in any school of Buddhism, but there are elements that are likely to feature in a marriage ceremony. A Theravadin couple may provide a meal for the monks on the morning of the wedding. At the service, they are likely to recite the Three Refuges and the Five Precepts. They may make vows to each other based on the teachings of the Sigalovada Sutta:

The bridegroom: 'Towards my wife I undertake to love and respect her, be kind and considerate, be faithful, delegate domestic management, provide gifts to please her.'

The bride: 'Towards my husband I undertake to perform my household duties efficiently, be hospitable to my in-laws and friends of my husband, be faithful, protect and invest our earnings, discharge my responsibilities lovingly and conscientiously.'

These vows may seem sexist to Westerners, but they would have been quite reasonable in ancient Indian culture. They are not intended to restrict people, but rather to emphasise ways in which a husband and wife can complement each other. Of course, there is no obligation to make them.

It is anticipated that Buddhist values and guidelines will ensure that a married relationship between two people will be happy and long lasting. However, it may be that problems occur, and these may become so serious that the couple considers separation and divorce. Buddhism is about overcoming suffering and not clinging to situations that produce suffering. Therefore, divorce may be preferable to living together unhappily. On the other hand, most Buddhists would consider divorce to be a last resort. They would feel it necessary first to examine the part they played in the breakdown of the relationship. Buddhists do not see weaknesses as failure, but rather as opportunities to find ways to develop strengths. They would, therefore, reflect on personal qualities (Paramitas) they may need to develop. They would want to avoid repeating their kamma in another relationship.

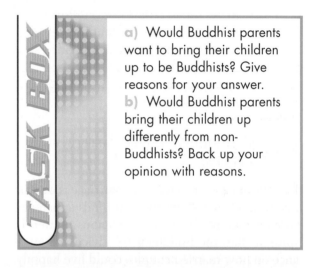

TASK BOX

a) Would Buddhist parents want to bring their children up to be Buddhists? Give reasons for your answer.
b) Would Buddhist parents bring their children up differently from non-Buddhists? Back up your opinion with reasons.

▲ A Buddhist wedding.

A New Approach – Buddhism

How might Buddhist parents bring up their children to share Buddhist values?

Even if a couple decides to get married, there is no obligation in Buddhism to have children. Yet if they do, they recognise the great responsibility they have for the life of another human being. It is their duty to lead their children away from evil, towards what is good, and to develop in them a pure mind. Children need to see their parents as good role models, and Buddhist parents will want their children to recognise the Six Paramitas in them. They will also want their children to learn the values of the Five Precepts. In putting the second Precept into practice, Buddhist parents will not interpret being generous as meaning spoiling their children by giving them whatever they want. Rather they will consider that their time is the most valuable thing that they can give.

The Sigalovada Sutta sets out duties and responsibilities that children have in relation to their parents. They are:

- To support them in their old age.
- To do as they are asked.
- To keep family traditions.
- To deserve their inheritance.
- To honour them after they have died.

Parents have a duty to show compassion for their children in five ways:

- By keeping them away from evil.
- By encouraging them to do good.
- By providing them with a good education.
- By making suitable marriage arrangements for them.
- By giving them their inheritance when they need it.

TEST YOURSELF

1 Why is there no established Buddhist marriage ceremony?
2 How might following the Five Precepts affect the relationship between a man and wife?
3 Which teachings might influence a Buddhist couple considering divorce?
4 How might the Sigalovada Sutta help settle family disputes?

WHAT IS THE BUDDHIST ATTITUDE TO WEALTH AND POSSESSIONS?

The path of Buddhism is the search for happiness (Nibbana). The Four Noble Truths teach that what prevents human beings from being happy, what causes them to suffer, is tanha – craving, wanting, desire. People rely on material possessions to make them happy, but Buddhism says that they are deluded. Material possessions cannot lead to happiness because of anicca: all things change, nothing is permanent. For this reason, Buddhist monks and nuns give up worldly things in order to live a spiritual life. Yet Mahayana Buddhists claim that anyone and everyone can become a buddha, whether they be monastic or lay believers. Lay believers need money in order to provide for themselves and their families. They need houses, cars, and all the material possessions that enable people to live in a civilised way in the modern world. At the same time, as Buddhists they wish to lead lives that bring spiritual fulfilment and allow them to reveal their buddha natures. The question, then, is this: is material wealth incompatible with the spiritual path? Is prosperity an obstacle to enlightenment?

An old man made his humble home outside a great palace. Those who lived in the palace were given every creature comfort: warm meals, fine clothing and private baths. The old man lived in a one-room hut he made himself, slept on an old mat and ate simply.

As the old man sat outside the palace eating his dinner of lentils and rice a guard came to see him. 'Foolish man,' he said. 'If you were to serve the king you could feast every night.'

The old man smiled and replied, 'Sir, if you were to eat lentils and rice you wouldn't need to serve the king.'

What is the message of this story, from a Buddhist point of view?

You need to think about the 'kings' people serve in the modern world. You should also think about Buddhist teachings on the Middle Way, tanha, and the happiness of Nibbana.

Evaluate the message by considering why some people would agree with it, why some people would disagree, and by basing your conclusion on these considerations.

▲ Is material wealth compatible with the spiritual path?

A New Approach – Buddhism

The Middle Way

The fourth Noble Truth states that the path to the happiness of Nibbana is the Middle Way. This refers to a life between the extremes of poverty and luxury. The Buddha taught that, just as the desire for wealth causes dukkha – suffering – so does poverty. Poverty, he claimed, is the cause of immorality, ill health and crimes such as theft, deceit, violence and corruption. He went on to say that if a ruler wants to reduce the rate of crime, he should not do it by making punishments more severe. He should do it by improving the wealth and living conditions of his people. The Buddha did not say that lay people should not enjoy their material possessions. On the contrary, he said that: 'These four kinds of happiness are appropriate for one who leads the household life [i.e. is not a monk or nun]. They are the happiness of owning things, the happiness of enjoying them, the happiness of being free from debt, and the happiness of honesty.'

Buddhism, therefore, teaches that being wealthy is not a problem. The problem lies in wanting to be wealthy. Wealth is not an end in itself, but a means to an end. Wealth for its own sake is the cause of unhappiness. Building up wealth at the expense of spiritual values will only bring suffering. The Buddha said, 'One who eats alone eats unhappily'. Yet wealth can bring happiness if it is used to create the conditions in which people can flourish. This means that money should be acquired through honest means (Right Livelihood), and used for the well-being of individuals, communities and societies. The important thing about wealth, then, is not how much a person has, but what they do with it.

Lay Buddhists, therefore, freely share their wealth with the monastic Sangha. In Theravadin countries, they contribute food, clothing and money in the belief that this is a good use of their money. Furthermore, in making these donations, they create punna (merit) for themselves, and this could be the cause of greater wealth. Mahayana Buddhists, too, are invited to contribute to monasteries and temples. Their donations help towards the upkeep of buildings and the preservation of Buddhist texts and treasures. They believe, then, that their money enables the Dharma to continue to spread, so their contributions are the source of good fortune. The Sutta says:

Wealth is neither good nor bad, just as life within the world with its sensual joys is neither good nor bad. It depends on the way the wealth is obtained and what is done with it, and in what spirit it is given away. People may acquire wealth unlawfully and spend it selfishly. Either case will not make one truly happy.

Instead one can acquire wealth by lawful means without harming others. One can be cheerful and use the wealth without greed and lust. One can be heedful of the dangers of attachment to wealth and share the wealth with others to perform good deeds. One can be aware that it is not wealth, nor good deeds, but liberation from craving and selfish desire that is the goal. In this way, this wealth brings joy and happiness. One holds wealth not for oneself but for all beings.

TEST YOURSELF

1 Describe the Buddhist attitude towards material possessions.
2 How, according to Buddhism, can wealth bring about unhappiness?
3 Why did the Buddha teach that poverty is good for bhikkhus, but not for lay believers?
4 How can the Five Precepts help Buddhists to make economic decisions?

HOW DO BUDDHISTS' BELIEFS AFFECT THEIR ATTITUDES TO ISSUES SURROUNDING BIRTH AND DEATH?

We have seen that one of the core beliefs of Buddhism is anatta: that beings have no fixed, permanent self; that they have an interdependence, which means each shares life with each other. Each life form has a kammic relationship with other life forms, so that actions made towards others are reflected back. One of the consequences of this belief is that Buddhists show their respect for life by showing compassion (karuna) for all living beings.

We have also seen that Buddhists believe that life consists of an endless cycle of birth, growth, decay, death and rebirth, which they call Samsara. As long as human beings create kamma, they must experience lifetimes to work through their kamma. Life is therefore eternal.

The purpose of the Buddhist Dhamma is to enable people to overcome suffering and experience perfect happiness. This means that actions that cause conflict are destructive, and therefore unskilful. Actions that cause harmony are creative, and therefore skilful. This is why the first Precept is against the taking of life and use of violence, instead promoting an attitude of loving kindness to all beings.

For Buddhists, these principles provide the context for discussion about issues concerning birth and death.

Abortion

The first Precept directs Buddhists not to take life. In the Patimokkha, the 227 rules for bhikkhus, one of the four most serious offences is the deliberate killing of a human being. The question, then, is this: is **abortion** the killing of a human being?

Under British law (except in Northern Ireland), human life starts at the moment a foetus is able to survive on its own outside its mother's womb. This time is called the moment of viability, and is currently settled at the end of the 24th week of pregnancy. As far as Buddhists are concerned, a person is reborn because of his or her kamma. Given that they believe that this working out of kamma is eternal, there is no point at which the embryo or foetus is not a living being. Therefore, Buddhists believe that a lifetime begins at **conception**, the point at which the egg is fertilised. It follows that they consider abortion to be the deliberate taking of a human life.

Buddhism teaches that killing is unskilful if:

- The object is a living being.
- It is known to be a living being.

▲ Humans share life in the same way fish share the water in which they swim. If you pollute it for others, you pollute it for yourself as well.

A New Approach – Buddhism

- There is intention to kill.
- The killing is active (i.e. the being is not left to die naturally).
- Death results.

Since Buddhists believe that life starts at conception, they also believe that abortion fulfils the five conditions, and therefore goes against the first Precept.

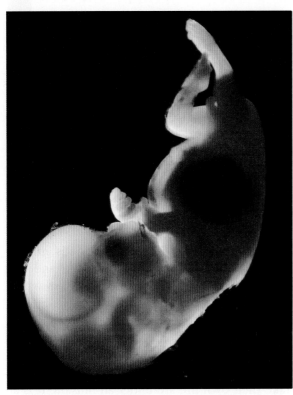

▲ **Buddhists believe that life exists from the moment of conception.**

However, we have seen that the Precepts are guidelines for moral action, and not hard and fast rules. Issues such as abortion are rarely clear-cut, and their complexity must be considered in making ethical decisions. If a woman is pregnant and is thinking about the possibility of having the pregnancy ended, all the factors of her unique circumstances must be considered. A Buddhist would apply the principle of upaya kausala (skilful means) in order to make her decision skilful. A skilful action is one that minimises suffering and maximises happiness.

It may be that pregnancy is the result of rape, and continuing with it would cause great mental and emotional suffering to the mother. It may be that the pregnancy is endangering the mother's life. In these cases, suffering is inevitable, whatever decision is made about abortion. Buddhists would feel compassion (karuna) for the mother in circumstances such as these and respect her decision.

Euthanasia

Euthanasia here refers to voluntary euthanasia, that is, the deliberate taking of a person's life, at their request, in order to end the suffering caused by a terminal illness. On the face of it, euthanasia fulfils the conditions of an unskilful killing: it is the intentional and active cause of the death of a living being. It therefore breaks the first Precept.

Yet the first Precept really guides against murder, and there are clear differences between murder and euthanasia. The two main differences are that euthanasia is motivated by love and compassion rather than hatred, and that voluntary euthanasia is carried out at the request of the dying person.

While Buddhists would agree that the motive for carrying out euthanasia may be love for the patient, most would deny that this love is Buddhist metta. Metta is love for all life. It could be said that it is love for life itself, which would include all living beings. Therefore, to cause harm to an individual being is to harm life itself. While the motive in carrying out euthanasia may be compassion for the individual, the intention is still to kill.

This does not mean that Buddhists would not feel compassion for those who suffer. On the contrary, Buddhism is about overcoming the suffering of all beings. Buddhists believe that it is possible for suffering to be overcome while the patient is alive. They support the provision of spiritual and medical care that allows a person to end his or her life in as painless and comfortable a way as possible.

The thirteenth-century Japanese priest, Nichiren, wrote to a follower of his who was gravely ill: 'Life is the most precious of all treasures. Even one extra day of life is worth more than ten million bags of gold.'

Do you agree? Give reasons to support your answer and show that you have thought about different points of view. You must refer to Buddhism in your answer.

The situation is rather different in cases of 'passive' euthanasia. Passive euthanasia is allowing a person to die naturally by withholding treatment that keeps him or her alive artificially. Here, no action is taken to bring about death, and therefore it is not unskilful. Indeed, it is said that Buddha himself had the option of extending his life when he became fatally ill, but decided not to. More recently, the Dalai Lama has said:

> In the event a person is definitely going to die and has virtually become a vegetable, and prolonging his existence is only going to cause difficulties and suffering for others, the termination of his life may be permitted according to Buddhist ethics.

Suicide

Many of the issues that apply to euthanasia apply also to suicide. Buddhist responses are therefore similar. In simple terms, suicide breaks the first Precept and is unskilful.

Buddhists would encourage someone who wanted to take their own life to reflect on those things that have caused the suicidal feelings. Buddhism encourages people to confront their problems with a calmness and wisdom that their religious practice gives them. It encourages people to develop patience (kshanti), courage and determination. It provides a way for people to overcome their suffering by overcoming the causes of it.

From the point of view of kamma, Buddhists consider suicide to be unskilful because it does not provide a way of overcoming or escaping from suffering. They believe that life does not end when the body dies, but rather that it continues by rebecoming at rebirth. Rather than bringing relief from suffering, suicide continues it, and is likely to cause more suffering for others.

Some people may claim that suicide is an individual decision to take one's own life, and that they should be free to do so. Buddhists would disagree. We have seen that they believe in anatta: no fixed or permanent self. All beings are interconnected and interdependent; each shares life with each other. Buddhism therefore says that those who claim that they should be free to take their own life are under an illusion. It is an illusion to believe that your life is your own. Life is not something to 'own', it is not a possession. Life, simply, is.

Therefore, Buddhists would feel compassion (karuna) for the mental or emotional suffering of someone contemplating suicide. They would recognise that such suffering can be overcome by a calm and peaceful mind. Buddhist meditation would create these conditions. Meditation has proved to be very successful in overcoming symptoms of clinical depression.

Belief in action: hospices

Hospices are places where people who are terminally ill may be cared for before they die. This usually means that they are given not only medical care to ease physical pain, but spiritual care to relieve emotional suffering. Hospice care may take place in the patient's home.

The Buddhist Hospice Trust is an organisation that offers help and support for the dying, their friends and relatives, and the bereaved. They do not offer medical or nursing care, but focus on catering for spiritual needs. Although they apply Buddhist principles in the support they give, they care for people of any religion or none.

The Trust has no paid employees and no premises. Supporters are all volunteers who visit patients in their homes, in hospital, or wherever they may be. Their aims are:

- To provide on request, where possible, spiritual friendship and compassionate care for those who are seriously ill, dying or bereaved.
- To provide information and other resources on Buddhist spiritual perspectives, cultural attitudes and practices surrounding death and dying, to Buddhists, healthcare professionals and the general public.
- To support a nationwide network of volunteers willing to offer spiritual friendship in their own localities.
- To encourage the practice of creating hospice in the heart – a personal opening to the reality of death, dying and suffering in the midst of life.

▲ The Buddhist Hospice Trust aims to provide compassionate care and companionship for the living, the dying and the bereaved.

They fulfil these aims by providing friendship and metta for those who are at the end of their lives and for their loved ones after their death. If they are asked to, they will give information and advice about death and dying from a Buddhist point of view. Supporters in each area are linked to each other in the Ananda Network. They take their name from Ananda, the Buddha's closest disciple, who cared for him as he died.

TEST YOURSELF

1. Which Buddhist principles may be relevant to a discussion about issues concerning life and death?
2. Why do not all Buddhists agree on a view about abortion?
3. Why are most Buddhists against euthanasia?
4. What advice might a Buddhist give to someone contemplating suicide?

WHY DO BUDDHISTS BELIEVE THAT ALL LIVING BEINGS ARE EQUAL?

In the time of Siddattha, society was divided into a hierarchy of **castes**. Each person had his or her own station in life according to the family they were born into. The highest caste was that of the Brahmins. This was the priestly caste, and Brahmins were powerful spiritual leaders. Next came the Kshatriyas, traditionally the caste of soldiers and civil servants. Then came the Vaishyas, the merchant class; and then the Shudras, the manual workers. Below these castes were people who did not belong to the caste system at all: the Dalits. They were, quite literally, 'outcastes', untouchables. They were separated from higher castes, and had to do the jobs that no one else would do.

Social inequality did not exist only in the caste system: there were also differences in the ways in which men and women were viewed and treated. Women were considered to be inferior to men. In fact, in the time of the Buddha, being born as a woman was thought to be a result of bad kamma. Being born as an untouchable or as a Brahmin, a man or a woman, was the consequence of actions performed in a previous lifetime, and their place in society was thought to be deserved.

Of course, this was a misinterpretation of the nature of kamma. It may be that being born male or female is a matter of kamma, but it does not follow that one is superior to the other. The caste system, on the other hand, was a social system, set up by human beings. The Buddha criticised the caste system, saying that a person should be respected for his or her actions, not social status: 'By birth one is not an outcaste, by birth one is not a Brahmin. By deeds alone one is an outcaste, by deeds alone one is a Brahmin.' Kamma is formed by skilful and unskilful actions, not by social class.

Buddhism, then, teaches that human beings are equal in terms of their social position. But it goes further: it says that all beings are equal, regardless of class, colour, religion, nationality, ethnicity or sex. The Buddhist belief in anatta – no fixed self – means that each being is connected with each other being. Everything is interdependent and affects everything else. A person's sex or skin colour is a temporary phenomenon within the wheel of Samsara. Indeed, the Buddha himself claimed to have been female in previous lifetimes. Tibetan Buddhists go further and say that everyone has been the mother of everyone else in previous lifetimes. Therefore, a person's race, nationality, colour or sex does not identify that person: there is no permanent identity.

Buddhism even teaches the equality of religions. The Buddha's final words were an encouragement for his followers to become enlightened, by whatever method they found most effective. 'Behold, bhikkhus, this is my last advice to you. All things in the world are changeable. They are not lasting. Work hard to gain your own salvation.' The Buddha compared life to a stormy sea, and religion to a raft. Any raft that serves its purpose and crosses the sea of suffering will do.

Every religion emphasises human improvement, love, respect for others, sharing other people's suffering. On these lines every religion has more or less the same viewpoint and the same goal.

Dalai Lama

From your studies of a range of religions, do you believe that they all share the same values, views and goals? You will need to provide evidence to support your opinion.

Buddhism teaches, too, that everyone deserves equal respect. The reason for this is that Buddhists believe that everyone has a buddha nature, the potential to be a buddha. Some would say that everyone is a buddha; it is just that they are not aware of it. When he became enlightened, Siddattha Gotama said, 'I now see that all beings everywhere have the wisdom and virtues of the Enlightened One, but because of misunderstandings and attachments they do not realise it.'

For the Buddha to say that all people have equal access to the buddha nature was revolutionary in Indian culture 2500 years ago. Women, in particular, regardless of their caste, were forbidden to study religious ideas and so would have no chance of learning how to meditate. Yet, during the Buddha's lifetime, the first Buddhist nuns (bhikkhunis) were admitted to the Sangha.

The first woman to request ordination was Mahapajapati, the Buddha's stepmother. At first, he was reluctant to agree. It is possible that he was testing her sincerity and determination to go against the strong Indian tradition that kept women away from the religious life. Or, perhaps, he was concerned that some women may want to become nuns just to raise their social status, since women had a very low position in society, and religious teachers had a high one. Nevertheless, Mahapajapati persisted. She shaved her head, dressed in brown robes, and encouraged 500 other women to do the same. They walked 300 miles to see the Buddha, who eventually allowed them to become the first bhikkhunis.

It seems that the Buddha was also concerned about the effect that women may have had on his male followers if they were to mix. It was possible that some may form relationships which would distract them from their spiritual path. On the other hand, he did not want the women to form a separate Sangha, where they may set themselves up to rival the bhikkhus. He therefore agreed to allow women to join the monastic Sangha, subject to eight rules.

Over the last 1000 years the number of bhikkhunis has dwindled. Today, there are so few that it is hard to believe that they will ever play a significant part in the monastic Sangha again.

Thousands of Hindus convert to Buddhism in India racism protest

PROTESTING AGAINST INDIA'S FAILURE to address caste issues at the World Conference Against Racism, thousands of Dalits – often classed as 'untouchables' in the Hindu caste system – converted to Buddhism in a northern Indian city.

Leaders of the late-Saturday ritual by some 6000 Dalits said they were protesting against discrimination by upper caste people and their government's failure to deal with caste issues. They said caste-based **discrimination** in India was as bad as racial discrimination in other parts of the world.

In Kanpur, 240 miles southeast of India's capital, New Delhi, hundreds of Buddhist monks in flowing robes arrived from Nepal, Japan and other countries to witness the ceremony, which was presided over by a Japanese Buddhist priest.

Participants distributed posters condemning Hinduism, the religion of India's overwhelming majority, whose beliefs are used to justify the caste system.

Dalits occupy the lowest rank in India's 3000-year-old caste system that discriminates against nearly a fourth of the country's billion-plus population.

Though India's Constitution, adopted in 1950, outlaws discrimination based on caste, the practice still pervades society.

▲ *The Associated Press*, 10 September, 2001.

WHAT DO BUDDHISTS THINK ABOUT WAR?

Although the Five Precepts are regarded as guidelines on how to live rather than rules, the first Precept is so fundamental to Buddhism that it is almost a commandment: do not take life. Buddhists tend not to become engaged in wars, and, in contrast to some other religions, violence has never been used to spread the faith. Nor is there animosity between different Buddhist groups. The Buddhist scriptures are full of references to the importance of peaceful relations between people:

Hatred never ceases through hatred in this world, but ceases through not hating only. This is an eternal law.

Dhammapada 5

The Buddha taught that his followers should never react with violence, no matter what is done to them:

Even if thieves carve you limb from limb with a double-handed saw, if you make your mind hostile you are not following my teaching.

Buddhism, therefore, teaches that violence between individuals can never be justified. But it is not blind to the fact that there are wars between nations, and there always will be. The Buddha teaches that, in times of war, his followers should act as peacemakers:

> Struggle must exist, for all life is a struggle of some kind. But make certain that you do not struggle in the interest of self against truth and justice. He who struggles out of self-interest to make himself great or powerful or rich or famous, will have no reward. But he who struggles for peace and truth will have great reward; even his defeat will be deemed a victory. In times of war, cultivate the mind of compassion, helping living beings abandon the will to fight.

The Buddhist principle of ahimsa says that non-violence is not just the position of not engaging in physical aggression or harming. It is, first and foremost, a state of mind. It is an attitude of peace towards one's environment. The constitution of UNESCO (the United Nations Educational, Scientific, and Cultural Organisation) states, 'Since wars begin in the minds of men, it is in the minds of men that the defences of peace must be constructed.' In this it echoes the words of the Buddha from 2500 years before:

> Mind is the forerunner of all evil states. Our life is the creation of our mind. If one speaks or acts with impure mind, suffering follows one as the wheels of the cart follows the ox that draws the cart.
>
> *Dhammapada 1*

On the other hand:

> Mind is the forerunner of all good states. Our life is the creation of our mind. If one speaks or acts with pure mind, happiness follows one as his own shadow that never leaves.
>
> *Dhammapada 2*

Buddhism is about being in control of your own life, not other people's. The Buddha therefore taught that the true battle is against the illusion of the self (anatta). A person who understands that everyone is connected has developed ahimsa.

TASK BOX

Imagine you live in a country that has conscription (compulsory recruitment into the armed forces). You are a Buddhist.

Write a letter to the Conscription Office explaining why you refuse to take part in war.

Remember: you are writing to someone who is unfamiliar with Buddhism, so you must explain carefully any technical terms that you use.

▲ How would a Buddhist deal with conscription?

A New Approach – Buddhism

What are Buddhist attitudes towards death and dying?

When the body is finally worn out, it dies. Again, for the Buddhist, death is seen as a natural part of life, but this does not mean that it is unimportant. On the contrary, it is a time to reflect on the changing and impermanent nature of things.

Of course, friends and family feel grief and sorrow at the death of a loved one, so Buddhists will exercise compassion and kindness towards each other. Death is also seen to be an opportunity for the bereaved to influence a favourable rebirth for the deceased. They pray to transfer punna – the merit they have built up – to that person.

PERSPECTIVES

Kisa Gotami

Kisa Gotami was the wife of a wealthy man. She had only one child. When her son was old enough to start running about, he became ill and died. Kisa Gotami was heartbroken. Unable to accept that her son was dead and could not be brought back to life again, she took him in her arms and went about asking for medicine to cure him. Everyone she encountered thought that she had lost her mind. Finally, an old man told her that if there was anyone who could help her, it would be the Buddha.

In her distress, Kisa Gotami brought the body of her son to the Buddha and asked him for a medicine that would bring back his life. The Buddha answered, 'I shall cure him if you can bring me some white mustard seeds from a house where no one has died.' Carrying her dead son, she went from door to door, asking at each house. At each house the reply was always that someone had died there. At last the truth struck her: no house is free from death. She laid the body of her child in the wood and returned to the Buddha, who comforted her and preached to her the Dhamma. She was awakened and entered the first stage of Arahantship. Eventually, she became an Arahant.

What does this story mean?

What do you think the mustard seed symbolises? Why?

What does this story teach about the Three Universal Truths?

Buddhist funerals

Buddhist funerals vary according to the school of Buddhism and the country where it takes place. In Thailand, Theravada Buddhists encourage a dying person to read or chant passages from the Suttas in order to create the kamma that will bring about a fortunate rebirth. After death, relatives pour water over a hand of the deceased. The body in its coffin is surrounded by light in the form of candles and incense. Sometimes, bhikkhus will come to recite passages from the Abhidhamma over it, and the family will present them with food so that they can create merit to pass on to the departed.

It is traditional in Buddhist societies to cremate dead bodies rather than bury them. This follows the ancient Indian custom that was practised on the Buddha. Cremation in Theravadin countries usually takes place three days after death. During this time, the body lies in the home where it can be visited by friends and relatives to pay their respects. This includes night-time vigils when people watch over the body.

On the day of the funeral, it is felt that the body should not leave the house in the way that a person normally would. It may therefore be carried out through a hole in the wall, but more often green leaves are placed on the floors and stairs to make the body's last departure from the house unusual. As the coffin is carried towards the place of cremation, it is led by community elders and bhikkhus. They carry a length of ribbon which leads back to the body in the coffin so that the dead person can continue to benefit from contact with the monastic Sangha. When the funeral procession arrives at the place of cremation, a service takes place during which the bhikkhus chant passages from the Suttas. The coffin is then placed on a pyre, and the mourners light a fire underneath it into which they throw incense.

In Tibetan Buddhism, it is traditional to read the Bardo Thodol to the dying in order to prepare them for the passage to their next lifetime (see p. 113). Monks continue to recite the Bardo Thodol and say prayers for 49 days after death to assist in this. The body itself may be cremated and put into a stupa if it was that of an important lama. But, in a country where fuel for burning is scarce, the corpse is traditionally offered to vultures in a ceremony known as **sky burial**.

Three days after death, the body is washed and put into the foetal position so that it leaves the world as it arrived. It is then wrapped in a white cloth and taken to the place of disposal. This is a walled area on a hilltop, usually near a monastery. The monks from the monastery will chant as they lead the corpse and procession of mourners to the place of disposal just before dawn. When the procession arrives, the corpse is unwrapped and body-breakers start to carve it into pieces. Juniper incense is burned to attract the vultures which are encouraged to eat it all. Even the bones are crushed up and mixed with flour for the birds to consume. In this way, it is believed that the deceased is taken to the Bardo.

It is thought to be spiritually healthy for people to attend a sky burial. They can confront the reality of death, and see in a most graphic way the impermanence of life. It is also a demonstration of the interdependence of all things as the vultures' bodies are nourished by the meat from the corpse. This in itself is believed to bring fortunate kamma to the deceased, for by sacrificing his or her body to the vultures, it is saving the lives of other creatures that may otherwise have been eaten.

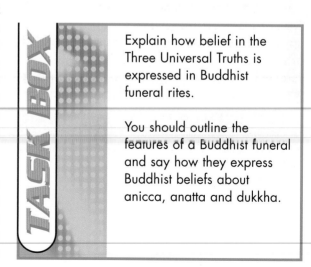

TASK BOX

Explain how belief in the Three Universal Truths is expressed in Buddhist funeral rites.

You should outline the features of a Buddhist funeral and say how they express Buddhist beliefs about anicca, anatta and dukkha.

TEST YOURSELF

1 What is Dhamma-care?
2 How do Buddhists keep the mind active in old age?
3 Describe what happens at a Buddhist funeral.

We should deal with nature the way we should deal with ourselves! We should not harm ourselves; we should not harm nature. Harming nature is harming ourselves, and vice versa. If we knew how to deal with our self and with our fellow human beings, we would know how to deal with nature. Human beings and nature are inseparable. Therefore, by not caring properly for any one of these, we harm them all.

HOW SHOULD WE TREAT THE ENVIRONMENT?

Following from the belief in anatta – no fixed self – is the belief that all things are connected and are interdependent. Therefore, Buddhists do not see the natural environment as being something separate from themselves. They believe that human beings are part of nature.

We, as human beings, have only just started to explore the ways in which our interaction with our environment affects both it and us. The relationship seems to be a kammic one, insofar as actions we make that damage our environment come back to harm us. On the other hand, actions we make to enhance the environment add to our happiness by enabling us to live more creatively and healthily. We expect nature to sustain us by providing resources for our food, for medicines, and so on; this will happen only as long as we contribute to the sustainability of the environment.

Some Japanese Buddhists call this relationship **esho funi**, which means 'humanity and the environment are two but not two'. In other words, although human beings and their environment appear to be distinct and detached from each other, they are, in reality, one. They exist in a state of mutual dependence. This means that humans have a duty to care for their environment for the well-being of the whole of the natural world. Caring for the planet is not doing something outside ourselves. For Buddhists, there is no outside. Thich Nhat Hahn, the Vietnamese engaged Buddhist, says:

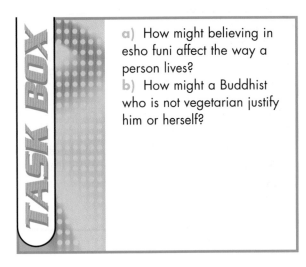

TASK BOX

a) How might believing in esho funi affect the way a person lives?
b) How might a Buddhist who is not vegetarian justify him or herself?

The first Precept guides against harming living things: all living things, not just humans. The positive aspect of this is to develop a peaceful mind (ahimsa) and extend metta (loving kindness) to all living beings. Yet the planet faces an ecological crisis because humans have taken from the environment in ways that are irreversible, and used those resources in ways that are damaging. This relates to the first two steps of the Noble Eightfold Path: we, as a species, have lacked Right View and Right Intention. Buddhism would say that the cause of the crisis is human ignorance of the nature of the interrelatedness of all things, and the greed that flows from that. Instead, humans should act with wisdom, compassion (karuna) and respect.

Individual Buddhists try to apply these principles to their daily lives. In living the Middle Way, they avoid the extremes of attachment to luxuries and suffering from hardship. This means that, as far as possible, they will use natural resources only to satisfy the basic needs of food, shelter, clothes and medicine. They will try to cater for what they need rather than what they want.

1   In what ways is our relationship with our natural environment kammic?
2   Describe what Nichiren Buddhists mean by esho funi.
3   How does an understanding of the Noble Eightfold Path help Buddhists form a view on conservation?

WEBLINKS

🕷 http://www.thubtenchodron.org/SchoolAndHome/
q_and_a_romantic_love_etc.html
Questions and answers about marriage and family life from a Tibetan monk in America.

🕷 http://www.buddhisthospice.org.uk/
Website of the Buddhist Hospice Trust.

🕷 http://www.ambedkar.org/
Website devoted to the Indian Buddhist, Dr Ambhedka, his work, his writings and his legacy.

REMEMBER

▶ Marriage has no religious significance for Buddhists.
▶ Buddhists do not believe that material possessions bring about dukkha (unhappiness).
▶ Buddhists do believe that tanha (craving material possessions) brings about unhappiness.
▶ Buddhists do not believe that having money is either skilful or unskilful.
▶ Buddhists do believe that how you spend your money can be either skilful or unskilful.

1 a) Describe in detail Buddhist teachings that would be relevant to a discussion about moral issues concerning birth and death. (8 marks)

b) Explain how a Buddhist might put ahimsa into practice. (7 marks)

c) 'It's your life: you should be free to do whatever you want to with it.'
Do you agree? Give reasons to support your answer, and show that you have thought about different points of view. You must refer to Buddhism in your answer. (5 marks)

2 a) Describe teachings about the responsibilities that Buddhists believe each person has for all living beings. (8 marks)

b) Explain how a Buddhist might work to make improvements in the world. (8 marks)

c) 'One individual cannot make a difference to the world.'
Do you agree? Give reasons for your opinion, showing that you have thought about another point of view. In your answer you should refer to Buddhism. (4 marks)

Assignment

Key Words

P = Pali
S = Sanskrit

Abhidhamma (P) **Abhidharma** (S)   A section of the Tipitaka that gives philosophical and psychological explanations of the Dhamma.

Ahimsa   'Not harming', non-violence.

Anapanasati   'Mindfulness of the breath' in samatha.

Anatta   No independent or permanent self.

Anicca   The impermanent nature of all things.

Arahant   In Theravada Buddhism, one who has attained Nibbana.

Bhavana   'Cultivation' or meditation.

Bhikkhu (Bhikshu – S)/**Bhikkhuni** (Bhikshuni – S): A Buddhist monk/nun.

Bodhisattva   'Enlightenment Being', one who seeks enlightenment for the sake of all beings.

Brahma viharas   The four sublime states: compassion, loving kindness, sympathetic joy for others, and even-mindedness.

Buddha   1. One who is fully awake or enlightened; 2. Siddattha Gotama.

Canon   The accepted Buddhist scriptures.

Chorten   A Tibetan stupa.

Dagoba   A Sri Lankan stupa.

Dana   'Generosity'.

Dhamma   1. The universal law of life; 2. The teachings of the Buddha.

Dhammapada   A Buddhist scripture containing 423 sayings attributed to the Buddha.

Dharmachari (m), **Dharmacharini** (f)   An ordained member of the Western Buddhist Order.

Dhyana   'Meditation'.

Dukkha   Suffering, unsatisfactoriness.

Engaged Buddhism   The use of Buddhism to help people by engaging mindfulness.

Enlightenment   The state of having developed the wisdom to see life as it really is.

Five Khandhas   The five elements that make up a human being.

Four Noble Truths   Suffering; the cause of suffering; the end of suffering; the way to end suffering.

Four Sights   Old age, sickness, death (i.e. suffering); a holy man (i.e. the determination to overcome suffering).

Gelong   A Tibetan Buddhist monk.

Hinayana   'Small Vehicle', a term used by Mahayana Buddhists for the Theravada school.

Jataka   'Lives', stories of the Buddha's previous lives.

Kamma (P) **Karma** (S)   1. Actions that influence one's future; 2. The law of cause and effect.

Karuna   'Compassion', sharing in the sufferings of others.

Kasina   An object of focus in meditation.

Kathina   A festival during which lay Buddhists donate robes to the vihara.

Kesa   1. A robe worn by a Japanese priest; 2. A scarf worn by Dharmacharis and Dharmacharinis.

Koan   A word or phrase intended to bring about satori in Zen Buddhism.

Kshanti   'Patience'.

Lama   A guru, or senior teacher, in Tibetan Buddhism.

Lhagtong   Vipassana in Tibetan Buddhism.

Mahayana   'Great Vehicle', the progressive Buddhist tradition of Eastern Asia.

Maitreya   The next Buddha for our world.

Mala   A string of beads used as an aid to mindfulness in puja.

Mandala   A pattern created to represent spiritual reality.

Mantra   A phrase chanted repeatedly during worship to evoke particular aspects of enlightenment.

Metta 'Loving kindness'.

Mitra A committed member of the Friends of the Western Buddhist Order.

Mondo Rapid questions and answers to bring about satori in Zen Buddhism.

Mudra Symbolic hand gestures used in Tibetan worship or on Buddha rupas.

Nembutsu Chanting 'Namu Amida Butsu' in Japanese Pure Land Buddhism.

Nibbana The state of peace achieved when suffering and its causes are overcome.

Noble Eightfold Path Eight steps towards overcoming desires and reaching Nibbana.

Pagoda A Burmese, Chinese or Japanese stupa.

Pansil The Five Precepts (short for Pancha Sila).

Patimokkha Rules for monks and nuns.

Pavarana Day A day when bhikkhus reflect on their behaviour during the Vassa.

Prajna 'Wisdom'.

Puja Worship.

Punna 'Merit', fortunate kamma.

Right Livelihood The principle that a person's employment should conform to Buddhist ethics.

Rupa 'Form', an image of the Buddha.

Samadhi State of deep meditation.

Samanera A novice, or trainee bhikkhu.

Samatha Meditation to establish calmness.

Samsara 1. The ordinary, ever-changing world; 2. The cycle of rebirths.

Sangha 'Assembly'. 1. The community of Buddhists; 2. The community of bhikkhus.

Satori 'Awakening', a flash of enlightenment in Zen Buddhism.

Sila 'Morality'.

Six Paramitas 'Six Perfections', virtues that lead a Bodhisattva to enlightenment.

Sky burial A traditional Tibetan funeral in which the corpse is exposed to the open air to be eaten by vultures.

Stupa Monument containing relics of the Buddha or important Buddhist teacher.

Sunyata 'Emptiness', the nature of things that have no fixed identity.

Sutta (P) **Sutra** (S) 'Thread', a text giving a teaching.

Tanha Desire, craving, wanting.

Tantra 'Pattern', mystic writings in Tibetan Buddhism. 1. The oneness of all things; 2. Techniques for visualisation.

Thanka In Tibetan Buddhism, a wall-hanging depicting the Buddha or an aspect of Buddhism.

Theravada 'The Way of the Elders', the main school of Buddhism in South-East Asia.

Three Poisons The causes of human unhappiness: greed, hatred, ignorance.

Three Refuges Devotion to the Three Treasures.

Three Treasures (Three Jewels) The Buddha, the Dhamma, the Sangha.

Three Universal Truths The characteristics of life: anicca, anatta, dukkha.

Tipitaka (P) **Tripitaka** (S) 'Three Baskets', the three collections of Buddhist texts: the Vinaya, the Suttas and the Abhidhamma.

Trikaya 'The Three Bodies', a way of explaining different aspects of buddhahood in Mahayana Buddhism.

Triple Gem The Three Treasures.

Upaya kausala 'Skilful means'.

Uposatha Day (Moon Day) The fortnightly recitation of the Patimokkha.

Vajra 'Thunderbolt', a symbol of power in Tibetan Buddhism.

Vajrayana 'Diamond or Thunderbolt Vehicle', a type of Mahayana Buddhism represented by Tibetan Buddhism.

Vassa The rainy season in South East Asia.

Vihara 'Resting Place', a Buddhist monastery.

Vinaya The rules of discipline for monks and nuns.

Vipassana 'Insight' meditation to see clearly the true nature of things.

Virya 'Energy'.

Wat A Thai Buddhist temple.

Wesak A festival to commemorate the birth, enlightenment and death of the Buddha.

Za-zen 'Sitting meditation' in Zen Buddhism.

Zhiney Samatha in Tibetan Buddhism.